The Essentials
of Horsekeeping

The Essentials of Horsekeeping

RACHEL HAIRSTON

Sterling Publishing Co., Inc.
New York

Disclaimer

This book contains the opinions and ideas of its author. It is intended to provide helpful and informative material on the subject covered. It is sold with the understanding that the author and publisher are not engaged in rendering professional services in the book. The reader should consult a competent professional for personal assistance or advice. The author and publisher specifically disclaim any responsibility for any liability, loss, risk, personal or otherwise, which is incurred as a consequence, directly or indirectly, of the use and application of any of the contents of this book.

Unless otherwise credited, all photographs are by Lyn Odom.

Library of Congress Cataloging-in-Publication Data

10 9 8 7 6 5 4 3 2 1

Published by Sterling Publishing Co., Inc.
387 Park Avenue South, New York, NY 10016
© 2004 by Rachel Hairston
Distributed in Canada by Sterling Publishing
^{c}/o Canadian Manda Group, One Atlantic Avenue, Suite 105
Toronto, Ontario, Canada M6K 3E7
Distributed in Great Britain by Chrysalis Books
64 Brewery Road, London N7 9NT, England
Distributed in Australia by Capricorn Link (Australia) Pty. Ltd.
P.O. Box 704, Windsor, NSW 2756, Australia

Manufactured in China
All rights reserved

Sterling ISBN 0-8069-8817-7

To my family

for their endearing love and support and

to all the horses

that have touched my life and taught me so much.

Contents

Preface

I hope that whether you've grown up around horses or are a first-time owner, the information in this book will help you maintain your horse's well-being and add to his quality of life. After reading this book, you may decide to change your horse's feeding or grooming routines, or you may consider building new housing facilities. Ideally, you'll be more aware of health risks, and you may even want to research the benefits of using holistic therapies along with traditional medicine.

A sound knowledge of horse care is essential. If you lack the ability to understand your horse's needs and don't take the time to learn the skills and practices necessary to care for him, you undermine his health, spirit, and ability to achieve optimum performance. Horsekeeping skills are not learned overnight. Most owners rely on the advice of knowledgeable teachers, such as family members, riding instructors, veterinarians, and trainers. By listening to their wise counsel and encouragement, every owner can become a great "horsekeeper," continuing to learn about horses. Good horsekeeping is more than just grooming and feeding. It's recognizing when your horse isn't behaving right or feeling well, understanding what excites him or scares him, being aware of how to keep his pastures safe, and knowing how to help him in an emergency.

This book was written to offer you a broader insight into what horsekeeping is really all about and to provide information to improve your horse's life through an effective and rewarding horse-care management program.

Acknowledgments

First and foremost, I want to thank my parents, Robert Crifasi and Sima Crifasi, for supporting my horse addiction and recognizing my deep connection to horses. My thanks and eternal love to my husband, Randy, for his patience, support, and encouragement throughout the process of writing this book and to my daughter Emma whose smile and laughter inspire me every day. Special thanks go to Madelyn Larsen, who turned my thoughts into complete sentences and navigated me throughout this project.

Many people and teachers have shared their knowledge and love of horses with me: Michael Korda, Senior Vice President and Editor in Chief at Simon & Schuster Inc.; Debra Hagstrom, Equine Specialist at the University of Illinois; Martha Vogelsang, Ph.D, Assistant Professor, Equine Sciences at Texas A&M University; Joann Kouba, Ph.D, Assistant Professor at Kansas State University; Jim Richardson, DVM; Madalyn Ward, DVM; Benjamin Espy, DVM; Texas A&M Animal Science and Equine Science Departments in College Station, Texas; and the John Bowne High School Agriculture Program in Flushing, New York.

For their patience and support and for graciously allowing us to photograph their horses, equipment, and facilities, a heartfelt thanks to Boerne Stage Saddlery in Boerne, Texas; Mumme's in San Antonio, Texas; Double Diamond Ranch in Boerne, Texas; Royal Legend Arabians in Bryan, Texas; Doe Creek Farms and Solitaire Ranch in Bandera, Texas; Side Hill Farm in Marble Falls, Texas; and Vanessa Felderhoff.

The Essentials of Horsekeeping

A horse gallops with his lungs, perseveres with his heart, and wins with his character.

—TESIO

Chapter 1

Housing Your Horse

Selecting a horse's living space is a big decision for any owner, but it doesn't have to be a stressful one. Planning your horse's ideal habitat should be a step-by-step process. Regardless of your financial situation, you can find safe, quality housing options for your horse. For the moment, set aside cost and space considerations and begin thinking about what lifestyle is best for your horse. Should it be an indoor or an outdoor one? The horse community has always disagreed on the best way to keep a horse. Everyone seems to agree that horses need time outdoors, but whether they need it 24/7 is another question. Some swear by barn life; others think it's just plain unnatural to keep a horse indoors for any length of time. The truth is, a horse can live safely and happily in both environments. In the end, you have to make the decision, based on what you think would be the right surroundings for your horse.

Finances, land, and building plans are discussed later in the chapter, but first, read about the differences in living in a barn and on a pasture. As you're reading, write down what you like and don't like about each option.

The barn

Horse owners say building a barn is more complex and more nerve-racking than building or buying their own home. Before hiring any building professionals, understand the structure and function of a good barn. Keep in mind what purpose the barn should serve for you and your horse. If you own and ride horses as a hobby, then a small, safe barn or shed would suit your needs. For something on a larger scale, such as breeding or training operations, you'll need to consider more comprehensive designs and building possibilities. You must consult with registered architects and professional builders on interior and exterior design, durable building materials, and, of course, the entire cost of

A well-designed barn provides good ventilation and allows horses plenty of visual stimulation.

the project. The main functions of the barn are to keep your horse safe, clean, comfortable, and protected from harsh weather, but the barn can also be a great place to store tack and feed, have an office, and provide a treatment area for vet care and farrier work. A barn can be a practical stable or an incredible equine showplace. Think about long-term plans and the possibilities of adding and making changes to the barn's design.

Basic barn structure

The following information on the components of a barn is simply for guidance. It is not a recommendation for a particular design or layout.

Roof

Clearly, the roof is one of the most important features of a barn. You can use a number of different materials, including aluminum, wood, and metal. Depending on your climate, the roof should be able to withstand heavy rain and snow and to provide proper drainage. If you want to be more stylish, you can build skylights into the roof for natural lighting. The roof should be well insulated and have vents installed to keep the barn well ventilated. The ceiling should be ten to twelve feet high to prevent a horse from injuring himself if he rears up in his stall or in the walkway. High ceilings also help provide good ventilation throughout the barn. Inadequate ventilation in a barn causes horses to develop respiratory problems, to experience difficulty cooling down on hot days, and to be more prone to certain bacterial diseases. In addition, the area under the roof can provide a good amount of space to build an office or an apartment for live-in staff. To accent your barn and improve ventilation, consider adding a cupola to the roof.

Layout

Once you and your architect have settled on the dimensions of interior space, you need to discuss your vision of the barn's interior. You will want to work on the details of arranging the location of the stalls, a wash area, and a tack or feed room. You'll even want to consider how much sunlight the barn should have in the morning. Try sketching some preliminary drawings for the architect. He or she should listen to your ideas and try to integrate them into the barn's design. As you sketch your design, remember that a stall is usually twelve by twelve feet, the interior walkway should be at least ten feet wide, and the barn doors should be about eight feet tall and open about four feet wide. The layout may have to change due to circumstances beyond your architect's or contractor's control. Try to be flexible and willing to compromise on other alternatives. The job of the members of your professional building team is to construct a safe and solid home for your horse, and their suggestions will help them do just that.

Creating a safe and healthy barn

Regardless of the size of the barn, the focus should be on keeping it clean, well ventilated, and most importantly, safe for the horses who live there and for the people who work and visit there. The floor should be durable, easy to clean, and safe for horses to walk on. Install a ceiling

Sweep the barn floors daily and leave doors open during mild weather to help air out the barn and reduce unpleasant odors.

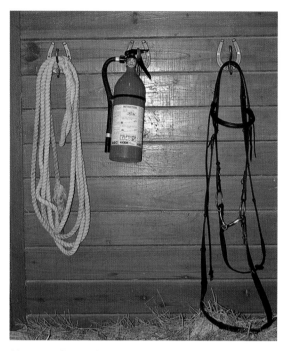

Mount a fire extinguisher where it is clearly visible in the barn. Perform regular monthly inspections and check the pressure indicator to be sure the fire extinguisher is in working order.

fan or a ventilation system to reduce unpleasant odors, circulate air, and keep the barn cool. If you live in a cold climate, consider installing a safe and efficient heating unit. Examine your lighting options to see whether you can use electrical and natural lighting together. Most electricians will be able to advise you about fixtures that are safe and durable. You want to install the most reliable electrical system available. Place lighting fixtures in areas where horses cannot come in direct contact with them. Keep barn walkways and main aisles free of clutter. Storage trunks and bins in walkways and in front of stalls are a safety hazard; place them elsewhere.

Install smoke detectors at strategic points around the barn. You'll need to mount at least two fire extinguishers on the walls where they are clearly visible from the barn walkway. Always have a fire evacuation plan ready and posted in the barn and in your home. Try to schedule occasional fire drills; time how long it takes to get all of your horses out. Having an organized emergency evacuation plan could save your horse's life.

To control flies, set up a permanent fly spray system. The liquid spray travels through pipes in the ceiling. Nozzles release the spray into the main parts of the barn. Usually, you can connect the system to a timer, allowing you to decide how many times a day it sprays. Other ways to control flies in the barn include flypaper, fly traps, regular manual spraying, and prompt manure removal throughout the barn. Consult your architect or contractor about a reliable drainage system to avoid indoor flooding and to remove any excess sewage and water.

Barn stalls

The roof is up, the supporting walls are secured, and large doorways welcome you into the barn. Planning to let your horses wander about freely? That's not a good idea. So, you need to plan the box stalls. The standard dimensions of a box stall are twelve by twelve feet and ten feet high. A stall this size gives most horses and ponies a good amount of space, but draft horses and warmblood horses need stalls that are fifteen by fifteen feet. The distance between the top of the stall and the ceiling should be at least two feet for safety and proper ventilation. Stall walls are typically paneled with strong wooden planks to protect them from kicks or strikes; concrete is not recommended because a strong kick directly onto concrete could seriously injure your horse. Clay is traditionally used for stall flooring, but you can also use dirt or rubber mats over concrete. Even with heavy bedding, the foundation floor should not be too firm.

The interior wall, or stall front, is usually the stall entrance. This is either open midway to the top or has metal bars spaced apart in the upper half of the wall. Either kind of stall front allows horses excellent ventilation and permits socialization with other horses. The exterior wall should have a minimum of a two-foot square window or another doorway leading outside to the paddock.

The stall door is a main component of the stall front design. Dutch

Dutch doors let your horse put his head outside his stall for some socialization time.

Sliding doors should open and close easily. They should have upper metal bars for increased ventilation and viewing.

doors have top and bottom sections that open independently. You can easily set a Dutch door in the exterior and interior walls for added accessibility. Many owners prefer a sliding door constructed of wood and metal bars, but this is only used as an interior stall door. All stall doors must have horse-proof bolts and locks to prevent a horse from unlatching them. At the same time, the bolts and locks must allow owners safe and easy access in and out of the stall. You can design a stall to open out into a connecting paddock, allowing a horse free access between his stall and the outside. The paddock doesn't have to be very large, just big enough to provide space for your horse to move around in safely. Of course, you can construct a paddock away from the barn within walking or trotting distance. This can range in size from ¼ acre to a full acre.

Inside the box stall

The inside of a basic box stall should have a waterer, feeder, buckets, mat, salt block, and bedding material. You can provide water with an automatic watering system or with buckets hung on the wall. Installing an automatic water system eliminates the chore of regularly filling water buckets and also eliminates any stagnant water problems. The drawback of using an automatic system is that you lose the ability to

Stalls must have at least two buckets for feed and water, fresh shavings, and a salt block.

gauge how much water your horse is drinking daily because the system refills constantly. For this reason, most owners opt to use two twenty-quart plastic water buckets. These are easy to fasten to the stall walls with brackets or special bucket hangers.

You'll need two types of feeders: one for grain and the other for hay. You can scoop grain into plastic buckets or rubber feed tubs placed on the floor or hung on the stall walls. Some feeders are triangular in shape; you can mount these in the corner of any stall. You can place hay in a hay rack; this is usually made of steel with safe, round edges. It is easy to mount on a solid wall. Place the hay rack at a comfortable level for your horse. If he must strain his neck to stretch upwards, he may choke. Never feed hay on the stall floor because your horse could eat shavings and manure along with the hay.

Salt is a vital mineral source in your horse's diet. Usually, owners place a salt block in a pasture or in a paddock, but if your horse's outdoor time is limited to the times when you are riding or training him, you should place a salt block in his stall. A mounted salt-block holder secured to the wall will prevent your horse from knocking the salt block over, covering it with bedding.

A stall should have rubber matting over the entire stall floor to provide a smooth, even layer of cushioning between the horse and the barn floor. Matting helps reduce dust buildup and prevents your horse from damaging his hooves when pawing.

Even a rubber mat should have bedding placed over it for additional padding and insulation. Wood shavings and straw are commonly used, but rice and peanut hulls are popular because they are safe, cheap, easy to clean, and absorbent. Wood shavings have a "clean" odor, are highly absorbent, very safe, and available in bulk quantities. Try to buy pine or cedar wood shavings; avoid black walnut or black locust shavings because they are highly toxic. Straw bedding is cheap and absorbent, but it is also very abrasive and dangerous if eaten by foals or young horses. Because horses can develop colic from eating straw bedding, horse owners are moving away from using it except when a mare is foaling. Hull bedding made from rice or peanuts is adequately absorbent but hard to spread evenly, and horses love to eat it and chew it. Sawdust has properties similar to those of wood shavings; but because of its fine granular form, you should not expose horses with respiratory difficulties or allergies to sawdust bedding. If you are planning to use sawdust from a local lumberyard, verify the type of wood to be sure the sawdust contains nothing that could be deadly if eaten.

Many new kinds of bedding have come on the market, including a biodegradable sterile wood fiber and a blended, natural granular clay. Both products have proven to be more absorbent, effective in small quantities, and successful in neutralizing odors than standard bedding materials. Woody Pet® Professional Bedding processes shavings and sawdust by extracting acids, tars, and oils and formulates them into a granular, sterile bedding product. When water or urine come in contact with it, the bedding changes from its granulated form to fluffy sawdust bedding that produces no negative effects. Stall Dry® is a unique blend of diatomaceous earth and clay that is easy to apply, pleasantly scented, and safe to use with all large animals. You can use it in stalls, trailers, barns, and on manure piles. Its granular form makes it easy to spread around the entire stall or on individual urine spots.

If your local feed or farm store doesn't stock the bedding you want, talk to the store manager about ordering it for you.

Mucking out the stall

At least twice at day, you should pick your horse's stall with a manure fork to remove manure and urine spots in order to reduce odors and flies. Try to leave as much clean bedding as possible by picking up only manure and urine spots with the manure fork. Spread the remaining

Rake or shovel urine spots and manure in stalls at least twice a day to control odors and flies. During the summer, do it three times a day.

bedding evenly around the stall. Place all stall waste into a cart or muck bucket and remove it from the barn. Set up a manure pile in an area away from the barn and grazing pastures. A horse produces up to eight tons of manure a year; it has to go somewhere. If you have a flower or vegetable garden, use the manure to fertilize soil and plants. Many local gardeners and garden clubs buy manure for their horticultural projects. Look into placing an advertisement, offering the manure for sale or for free, depending on how eager you are to get rid of it. Plan on doing a strip-down cleaning of the stall every four weeks in the summer and every six weeks in the winter. This means taking out any bedding, removing and disinfecting the rubber mat, and washing the stall walls and floors with either hot, soapy water or a safe disinfectant. Cleaning stalls at set intervals will control the mold, bacteria, and flies in your barn.

Foaling stall

A foaling stall is located in a segregated area of the barn. As the name implies, its purpose is for foaling. It is also used as a nursery for your mare and foal. It should be kept clean with straw bedding and only be used by broodmares. If you are using wood shavings, be aware that they can be breeding grounds for bacteria. You should clean them out regularly for the foal's safety. You'll need to clean out the stall every two weeks, even if it is not in use, to prevent any buildup of dust, mold, or germs. Bring the expectant mare into the foaling stall three weeks prior to her estimated foaling date. This will remove her from her stable-mates and allow her time to become acclimated to her new environment. Keep supplies for the foaling close by, either in a trunk or storage area next to the stall. When designing your barn, locate the foaling stall in a quiet, clean area and not next to another stall. If you plan to breed more than three mares a season, consider building two foaling stalls.

Storage space

Designing a barn with no storage space is usually the biggest mistake made during the building process. A good architect will help you construct some type of storage area for current and future use. It doesn't have to be fancy or expensive, and it can even be condensed into one room for all your tack, feed, and other equipment. For storing items such as tools, paint, and nails, consider constructing a storage shed separate from the barn. This will leave more space for other requirements inside the barn. It is also safer to keep these items away from the barn. Typically, a tack room and feed room are separate spaces since they serve different purposes, but they don't have to be very large or intricately designed in order to meet your needs.

Tack room

Store tack, such as saddles and bridles, in a clean and dust-free environment. Because of the amount of money you've invested in a good saddle and bridle, you'll want to keep them in top condition. Consult with your architect about the size of the room, basing your decision on how much tack you have and how much open space is left. You can create an attractive and functional tack room if you use all of the space to your advantage. Utilize wall space by mounting different types of racks and brackets. Steel-reinforced saddle racks are very sturdy, can hold any type of saddle, and fold down against the wall when not in use. You can easily move a wooden or metal saddle stand around the room; it, too, folds down for storage. Although it takes up floor space, it's a nice alternative to wall racks. Wall-mounted semicircular racks hold bridles and halters correctly to keep their shape. Bridle and halter brackets are not as elaborate as the racks, but they are inexpensive and a good choice if you are on a budget. You can mount a large towel rack on the wall for storing saddle pads or blankets or for drying them after you've washed them.

This is a well-organized tack room. Mountable saddle racks are perfect for utilizing wall space and maintaining the saddle's shape.

Setting up a tack room doesn't have to be expensive; most organizers cost between three and twenty dollars each. Tack, home, and storage supply stores have large assortments of accessories and hardware from which to choose. For other ideas, consider looking at tack rooms in local boarding stables, breeding farms, and training stables. The staff at tack and saddlery stores can offer great advice on tack room design. They are usually very happy to help you choose the right storage tools.

Feed room

Think of the feed room less as a room and more like a vault. Feed, grain, and hay need to be stored in a safe, cool, and clean area. You must keep insects, birds, and rodents away from your horse's feed. They eat his food and contaminate what is left with feces and disease. A good feed room should have solid walls, a concrete floor for easy cleaning, and a steel-framed, lockable door with a rubber strip along the bottom to seal it off from any pesky critters and hungry horses. Ideally, you should keep the room cool and maintain a low level of humidity since hot temperatures and excessive moisture cause hay and grain to lose their palatability. You can store grain and concentrates in plastic garbage cans with locking lids and in metal grain bins with padlocks.

Large plastic trash cans are ideal for storing concentrates, chopped forage, and treats.

For a smaller barn, companies like Rubbermaid® make plastic garbage cans on wheels. These hold thirty to fifty gallons and have handles that lock the lid down. No animal can gnaw through or open these cans, and the feed is safe and clean inside. Store each type of feed separately in its own can, clearly labeled on the outside. If you board your horse, buy a can to store your grain and write your horse's name all over it. A larger barn should consider using metal bins with locks. These bins can hold a much larger quantity of grain than the plastic cans and are equally effective in keeping out rodents and insects.

Hay storage can take up a hefty amount of space in the feed room. Ask the architect or contractor to calculate how many bales of hay can fit in the feed room along with feed cans and bins. Since most hay is sold by the bale, only buy what can fit into the feed room. To store larger quantities of hay, consider creating a hay storage area separate from the feed room. Hay does not have to be stored in a separate room, just kept in a dry area of the barn with a plastic tarp covering to prevent moisture buildup and to reduce storage loss.

Hot walkers

Horses that spend most of their time in a stall need to have some daily exercise. Even if you can't ride that day or no pasture or paddock time is available, your horse needs a minimum of thirty to forty-five minutes of exercise a day; a hot walker is a good alternative. This mechanical device walks or trots a horse around in a circle. It is a staple at every Thoroughbred breeding farm. A small motor moves the sixteen- to twenty-foot long arms of the umbrella-shaped walker at a steady pace. You snap the leadline clip, found on the end of the hot walker's six- to eight-foot high arms, to the side buckle of your horse's halter. When turned on, the walker moves the horse forward. In general, a hot

A hot walker is a safe and convenient way for your horse to get daily exercise when you can't ride him or turn him out to pasture.

walker is safe, but you still need to check on your horse when he is on one of them. An ordinary hot walker has two speeds: for a slow walk and trot. More expensive models offer four speeds, including a fast walk and trot. In order to avoid serious injury, no horse should ever canter or gallop on a hot walker. More importantly, the hot walker should have a safety gear or device that automatically shuts off the motor when a horse falls down. You can place a hot walker in a paddock and install a canopy above it.

Some options to consider when buying a hot walker include the number of horses able to walk at the same time, speed requirements, safety features, cost, and the manufacturer's warranty. The hot walker is not meant to be your horse's only source of exercise. It is ideal for occasional use when you are unable to ride or want to supplement your horse's exercise and conditioning program. Because it is expensive, think carefully about how it fits into your horse's training, if at all. Walking or riding your horse for just thirty minutes a day will give you both some exercise and great bonding time together.

Pasture living

Keeping your horse on a pasture seems easy enough. Just put up a fence and let him graze to his heart's content. Right? Wrong. You have a lot

Pastures are a living space and a constant source of roughage. On a high-quality, large pasture, your horse can meet all his exercise and dietary requirements.

to think about before letting your horse live out on your pasture. The first step is to decide where you want the pasture to be. For safety and convenience, think about building the main pasture close to your house. It doesn't have to be right outside your door, but the pasture's entrance shouldn't be too far away. When choosing the land for a pasture, give thought to these issues: Can you build more than one pasture for rotational purposes? What building plans do you have for the pasture in the next five to ten years? Is it free of poisonous plants and grasses? Are there trees for shade and a natural water source? Do you have a manure disposal plan in place? You have lots to think about in order to protect your horse's safety and well-being.

Land quality

The quality of the land you want to use for pasture is an important consideration when deciding whether to keep your horse on pasture all year round. The pasture's grass must be rich in vitamins and minerals, nontoxic, and fast growing. Many local agricultural agencies will identify the species of your grass and analyze it for nutrient content. The grass you have should be safe and easy to digest, such as coastal, Bermuda, or ryegrass. Remove highly poisonous plants including yew, oleander, water hemlock, jimsonweed, and tall fescue. Trees inside the fence line and just beyond it should provide excellent shade and must be safe in case your horse eats the bark or leaves. Black locust, black walnut, elderberry, red maple, and horse chestnut are considered highly toxic to horses. Because a horse could choke on fruit and nuts, avoid having trees that produce them in the pasture. It's a good idea to invest in a field guide with color photographs so you can walk around the pasture and identify plants and trees.

You'll need a comprehensive soil analysis to test for pH levels and mineral content. Your local agricultural agency will do this. To maintain a high quality in the soil, have a sample tested at least every two years. If the grass in your pasture is unhealthy, slow growing, or vitamin deficient, select another area to build a pasture.

Excessive amounts of water and flooding can damage and destroy healthy grass. Adequate drainage, either natural or constructed, is necessary to prevent your horse from living in a muddy swamp. A contractor can advise you about installing a drainage system to remove excess water and about the drawbacks of setting up a pasture on land prone to puddles and mud after rainstorms. Look for slightly hilly areas with natural slopes to drain and absorb water produced by heavy rainfall or melting snow. All areas of the pasture should be carefully inspected for rodent or snake infestation as well as any unsafe holes or exposed tree roots. You should perform a routine check of all pastures at least every three months. You may want to do it weekly or monthly, depending on the size of your property. Regular assessments of all active pastures will ensure a safe and healthy living space for your horse.

Feeding on pasture

Most active horses will get 50 percent of their daily feed requirement from grazing. Older horses will meet 90 to 100 percent of their daily nutritional needs from pasture grazing by consuming 1 to 3 percent of their body weight. For pasture horses, grazing forage is a major source of their diet. Again, if you are unsure about the type of grass on your land, have a sample identified by your local agricultural authorities. You must rule out any potentially dangerous grasses, such as kleingrass, fescue, and johnsongrass. If you are using concentrates or grains to supplement the diet of active, young horses, you will need a pasture feeder that is heavy, sturdy, and easily accessible. A standard pasture or corral feeder is a deep plastic bucket easily mounted onto a fence. You can find single feeders or double feeders to hold between thirty and sixty pounds of feed. Many owners use a tire feeder in pastures because it is very durable and difficult for horses to push over, decreasing the loss of feed. You can place a bucket or feed pan inside the center opening of the tire, which holds it securely in place. For a simpler feeder, tie a bucket or buckets to a fence or hang them on a fence-post bracket. In addition to a feeder, place a salt block on the ground or in a holder mounted on the fence.

Forms of pasture shelter

During hot, sunny days, healthy trees provide a sufficient amount of shade, but during the colder months their bark and limbs invite chewing. The trees in your pasture should be nontoxic, and they should not produce sap. Regular removal of chewable branches and dangerous limbs keeps the trees healthy and the horses safe. To discourage bark chewing and to protect the trees, wrap thin mesh wire around tree trunks, limiting access to them. Be sure to secure the wire. If you don't have enough shade trees, build a walk-in shed or shelter to provide shade and protection during bad weather. A covered shelter is usually a frame structure without walls or with walls on only three sides. You can build a shelter in less time and for less money than a barn. When building a covered shelter:

◆ Allow one hundred square feet per horse.
◆ Select a well-drained area.

Pasture and paddock shelters can be simple, walk-in sheds with open sides and a large roof. They are inexpensive to build and allow horses free access to shelter.

A more elaborate type of pasture shelter has several aluminum pipe stalls with open sides underneath a full roof. In warmer climates, it's an excellent alternative to a barn.

◆ Eliminate exposed bolts or loose metal.

◆ Build the roof to slope away from the opening.

◆ Orient the shelter so that the opening faces south.

◆ Design the opening to be a minimum of ten feet wide or design the structure to be open on all sides.

◆ Consult an architect or local contractor to make sure any proposed pasture shelter is designed and built correctly. That includes building it in the right place, with the proper drainage, and with the best materials. A covering does not have to cost a lot of money; whatever you spend is an investment in protecting your horse.

Water sources

A natural water source, such as a pond or creek, is ideal for a pasture because it provides quality water at no cost. Creeks and streams are perfect since they are free flowing, limiting the buildup of bacteria and algae. Ponds, on the other hand, can become stagnant and produce an overgrowth of algae that can cause digestive problems in horses. You can put goldfish in your pond to control the algae population naturally.

A natural water source means less work for you; however, if you don't have a natural water source in the pasture, you'll need to make a pond or water tank. You can use a hose to connect either one to a separate well water source or to an existing water system and fill it manually when needed. Water tanks usually hold anywhere from fifty-five to one hundred gallons of water. Releasing the drain plug allows you to clean them. You should thoroughly drain and clean a water tank once a week. One horse drinks an average of eight to twelve gallons of water daily, so a safe and clean water source is a top priority. If you live in a cold climate, place a specialized tank-warmer inside the water tank to prevent freezing. The warmer contains a thermostat to activate it when the temperature drops below 40 degrees F.

Fences

Once you've inspected the pasture and consider it safe, you can think about the fencing you will need to protect your horse. Fences vary in both performance and price. They must be at least five feet high and clearly visible to your horse. A horse can seriously injure himself if he runs into a fence. The odds of this occurring increase if the fence isn't visually distinct. Think about what type of fence is best for your pasture in terms of maintenance requirements, installation and repair costs, and safety. As with any long-term plans for the pasture, confirm that you can upgrade and expand the fencing system you select. Once you determine the type of fence you want to use, decide whether to install the fence on your own or to pay someone else to do it for you. Installing a fence is not an easy job and, if you have no building experience, hiring a professional may be a wise choice. Some contractors and fence distributors will give you a price quote that includes materials and installation. Fencing prices are quoted by the foot with posts at a certain distance; the price includes rails or wires. Shop around, contact fence manufacturers for brochures, and talk to installers who will work within your budget. The American Fence Association (AFA) can answer some of your questions and refer you to a local AFA professional. Their toll-free number is 1-800-822-4342. The most common fences on the market today are wood, electric, wire, and vinyl.

Wood fences

Wood fences come in different styles, such as post-and-board and post-and-rail, and are relatively inexpensive to buy and install. Expect to pay between five and eight dollars per foot installed. You'll pay more for wood that has been treated or painted for longevity. A wood post-and-board fence can be three or four planks high with about a foot of space between the bottom plank and the ground. Similarly, a post-and-rail fence is three rails high with a foot between the last rail and the ground. Boards should be about six inches wide with four-inch posts every ten

Post-and-board wood fences are the most common type of fencing because they are strong, inexpensive, and freely available. However, they require more maintenance than other types of fencing, such as electric and vinyl.

feet. A good post-and-board fence can last about fifteen years if well maintained.

The main drawbacks of a wooden fence are the damage bored horses can do when they chew on it and the expense of repairing or replacing it. Running an electric wire along the interior section of the top rail or board discourages horses from chewing on the fence. Because wooden fences are so vulnerable to damage, they may require constant painting and staining. One way to reduce your costs is to consider white, vinyl-coated, wood post-and-board fences. These deter chewing, require very little upkeep, and cost about seven dollars per foot for a three-board fence. Vinyl coating is very effective in protecting the wooden structure underneath, but you'll need to check for cracks to prevent corrosion from rainwater seepage.

Electric

Electric fencing comes in several different forms. You can choose from electric rope, coated high-tensile wire, electric braid, or electric tape. Each works by conducting a constant electrical current that mildly shocks the horse when he pushes up against the fence. Usually after a few jolts, a horse avoids the fence entirely. All these fences consist of three to four rows of wire strands tightly attached to wood or steel posts

The electric fence is a safe and practical alternative to wood and wire fences. Its mild, humane shock discourages horses from leaning or pushing against the fence.

and connected to a charger that supplies electricity. Depending on the type you select, a fence charger costs from fifty to five hundred dollars. Before investing in an electric fence, review the electricity rates in your area. Although an electric fence requires minimal maintenance, the cost of keeping it activated 24/7 could mount up over the course of a year.

The advantages of an electric fence include the low cost of the materials and the ease of installation. The cost of these fences ranges from one to three dollars per foot, not including the charger. Electric fences vary in appearance, the amount of space between posts, and pounds of tension per wire. They work well in combination with other fencing materials, such as wood and vinyl. Most electric fence companies back their product with a twenty-five-year warranty and testimonials from satisfied customers. In making your decision, remember that the shock is very mild and humane, just enough to get the message across. Electric fencing is safe and effective.

Wire fences

When people think of wire fences, the first one that usually comes to mind is barbed wire. Because it is dangerous around horses, you should never use it for fencing. This doesn't mean that all wire fencing is dangerous; some wire fences can be a suitable alternative to electric and vinyl ones. Coated, or smooth, thick wire strands can be set up in three rows that are secured to metal posts. These are normally not as durable as other types of wire fences.

Woven wire and narrow-mesh fences are safe options with minimal maintenance. On average, expect to pay three to five dollars per foot for woven wire installed and six to eight dollars for narrow-mesh wire

Wire fences are fine for less active and younger horses, but they do not work as well for stallions or very active horses. Never use barbed wire or wide-mesh wire.

installed. With these types of fencing, the wires are nailed or stapled to wooden "sight" boards. The sight boards are very similar to the post-and-board arrangement; top and bottom boards attach to two posts, and sheets of wire are installed between the two boards. Both kinds of wire fences are very durable, require little maintenance, and are easily visible to your horse. However, they are not always easy to install. Consider hiring a professional builder to construct and install a wire fencing system.

Vinyl (PVC) fencing

Vinyl fencing has gained great popularity among horse owners. Although it is more expensive than other fences, it is worth every penny. According to manufacturers, vinyl is a safe, attractive, durable, and maintenance-free fence that horse owners love. The synthetic fence, constructed of polyvinyl chloride (PVC) and resins, resists high ultraviolet rays that cause corrosion and damage. In addition, it is weatherproof, termite resistant, colorfast, and not chewable. PVC fences come in two to six rail/board versions in the post-and-board or rail style. Vinyl-covered wood is a less popular form that comes in a post-and-board style with three to four board selections. Unlike pure PVC fencing, vinyl-covered wood may suffer some water damage if water

Vinyl fences are well worth the money because they are low maintenance, safe, and extremely durable. Many owners choose white **PVC** fencing because it adds style and harmony to their farm's borders.

seeps through a crack in the coating. Both kinds of vinyl fencing cost seven to ten dollars per foot installed. Investing in a vinyl fence is a wise and economical choice since it saves money in maintenance and usually comes with a twenty-five-year or lifetime warranty. Each company has several styles and colors; most companies offer free brochures and provide a website on the Internet for additional information.

Pasture management

Maintaining the quality and safety of any pasture requires an effective and regular management program. Since a pasture serves as both a nutritional source and a living space, its upkeep needs to be a priority. Be conscious of the number of horses turned out onto one pasture and of each of their dietary needs. Rotate pastures weekly or monthly to prevent overgrazing; only allow your horses to graze the grass down to two inches. Letting horses graze down to the dirt is not nutritionally beneficial for them, and it isn't good for the grass. In order to have top-quality grass, never turn horses out onto a pasture before it has reached its full potency; wait at least one entire maturing season before using it. Once you rotate horses to another pasture, mow the grass to keep it level and use a harrow to spread and break up manure piles. Continue to check the nitrogen (N), phosphorus (P), and potassium (K) levels and adjust accordingly. You must watch pastures for toxic plants and forages, insects and rodents, and holes or exposed roots. After severe storms, always check pastures for fallen tree branches and deep mud holes that could injure your horse. Keep in mind that a healthy pasture means a healthy horse.

Planning your horse's living space

Now that you know more about barns and pastures, start imagining which is best for your horse. Horses are adaptable animals, and that makes your job as an owner much easier when it comes to choosing a space. After reading about barns and pastures, perhaps you have jotted down what you liked and didn't like about each. If so, those notes will become helpful as you move into the planning phase. Your options are indoors, outdoors, and a combination. Begin the planning process by taking a realistic "inventory" of what you have so that you'll know what you need and what it will take to build your horse's ideal living space. Make a chart with the following topic headings: acreage, finances, quality, climate, and zoning. Go through each topic, making entries in the chart. These entries will give you a starting point toward building a great space for your horse.

Acreage

The first issue to tackle is how much quality acreage you can completely dedicate to your horse. Ask yourself if you can build the facilities you want on the acreage you have. Is there enough acreage for a barn with pastures or a nice-sized shelter on the pasture? Ultimately, a professional is best qualified to answer these questions, but before consulting one, decide approximately how many acres are for horse use only and identify which ones you want to use. Once you've decided on the potential pastures, determine if they can meet your horse's grazing demand and provide plenty of exercise space. If your horse is only on a pasture diet, you need ten to fifteen good-quality acres divided into two or three fenced pastures. Plan on having more than one pasture for rotating purposes. If your horse is on both a pasture and grain diet, then six acres divided into two pastures will be sufficient. Obviously, the more land your horse can feed and exercise on, the better. If you have a limited amount of land, dedicate at least one acre of high-quality fenced pasture per horse and consider supplementing the feed with concentrates and extra exercise. On the "acreage" section of your chart, write down approximately how many acres you have chosen.

Finances

The next step involves expenses. Horse owners want the best facilities for their horses. Some owners even go into serious debt to provide it. Review your budget carefully; decide on an amount you can realistically spend. Plenty of options are available regardless of the size of your budget. If you are determined to build a barn and have limited funds, begin investigating property refinancing plans, loans, and private payment plans through contractors and barn manufacturers. Many owners build a small barn or shelter initially, planning to add on to it later when they can afford to do so. For an accurate budget and financial evaluation, meet with an accountant or financial planner who can help you decide how much money you can afford to use, how to obtain additional funds, and what tax laws or federal assistance may be available. Never undertake any building project without a firm budget or you could end up with a disaster instead of a barn or pasture. With an accurate financial statement in hand, start thinking about the next step. Do you want to spend funds on a barn or on a shelter in a pasture? Which is more cost effective, small paddocks close to the barn or several fenced pastures? Building a barn is no longer a simple matter of getting some wood and asking a bunch of neighbors to help you. A barn is a major construction project that requires the services of an architect and a contractor whose fees need to be considered in addition to all the building materials. Try to get several estimates and referrals from other horse owners. Interview experienced building professionals who specialize in horse facilities and barn construction.

When building a shelter, you should only hire a contractor who is licensed and bonded. Most contractors can show you prior work, offer references, and stay on budget. In addition, your contractor should feel that building a shelter is just as important a project as building a barn. If your plan is to build only fenced pastures, invest in good-quality fences and hire a reputable installation company that offers warranties and repair service plans. No matter what you choose to do, always remember that expensive is cheap, and cheap is expensive. Use your money wisely, but don't cut corners on safety, durability, or experience. Once a budget is finalized, write down the amount chosen in the "finances" section of your chart.

Quality

The quality and species of grass and trees on your land will be a key factor in deciding if your horse can live on the land allocated for him. Of course, fifteen acres would be a great space for him to gallop around in, but not if the area has unhealthy trees, poor grass quality, or poisonous plants. Once the local agricultural agency has performed a full inspection of the grass and trees on the property, identified any dangerous species, and tested the soil, you will get an accurate report on what needs improvement. This may include replanting, rebalancing soil content, and removing certain grasses, trees, and plants. For the benefit of your horse, do whatever it takes to ensure that the land is safe and supports his needs. If the pasture cannot meet all his nutritional requirements, supplement his diet with concentrates and vitamins. Turning out your horse onto a pasture without knowing what type of grasses and trees are growing on it could be a fatal mistake. In the "quality" section of your chart, write a general description of the grass; put a check by it after you have had it inspected.

Climate

If you live in an area prone to cold, rainy, and snowy weather, a barn is essential for your horse's safety and comfort. Horses are very hardy animals, but they need adequate and durable shelter during extreme weather conditions. Barns for one to twelve horses, covered shelters in pastures, or even large trees out in a field can supply some form of safe haven from harsh weather. Again, you should consider consulting a building professional who will take climate and weather into consideration when designing and building your horse's living space. For many owners, a barn is the best housing option for their horses during harsh fall and winter seasons. Owners living in warmer climates with milder weather usually build covered shelters instead of full barns. Even with the best ventilation, some barns can be stifling heat traps in hot climates. A large covered shelter can provide plenty of shade, but you need to be sure it can protect all the horses that will need access to it. Well-pruned trees around the pasture provide additional areas of cooling shade. Think about the weather in your area over the past few years, speak to neighboring horse owners, and decide how important a role the weather plays in protecting and keeping your horse healthy. In the "climate" section, write down the most common weather conditions as well as the average high and low temperatures for the past year. To get accurate temperatures, contact your local agricultural agency or the National Weather Service for detailed weather records.

Zoning

Zoning laws dictate how and where you can keep a horse. Before signing any contracts, contact your local government to obtain the zoning regulations and laws for your area. Learn about local zoning laws, ordinances, and required permits pertaining to horses, livestock, fences, barn structures, commercial use, and land use. You can also consult a reliable real estate lawyer who knows the local zoning laws and can safely guide you through the process of buying or improving a horse property. Architects and contractors usually know the zoning laws and can advise you about what can and cannot be done. It's easy to rush into buying or building on a new property. Be restrained and get good advice first to avoid a lawsuit and a possible loss of money. When looking to buy a horse property, choose a real estate agent who understands your plans and visions. To save you from future headaches, consult a lawyer before signing any contracts. Once you have met all zoning laws and regulations, place a check in the "zoning" column.

Hiring professionals

With the information you have regarding acreage, finances, climate, land quality, zoning, and housing preference, start asking other horse owners for referrals to architects and builders. Check local horse newspapers and contact professional associations for the names of certified and licensed members in your area. In addition to these sources, local agricultural agencies and veterinarians have information about builders, distributors, and manufacturers of horse facilities.

When you have compiled a list of candidates for the job, you can begin interviewing them. Select the ones who will build what you want and not what they want. Be sure to get estimates and review all contracts carefully before committing to the project. Use your lists as guidelines to help communicate exactly what you want to your building team. Ideally, the end result will be a perfect living space for your horse.

Boarding your horse

If you don't own enough property or if your land is not zoned for horses, consider keeping your horse at a boarding stable. Many horse owners board their horses because it suits their lifestyle. For a monthly fee, they have access to excellent riding facilities and a full-time staff caring for their horse. In addition, they don't need to invest time or money in building their own stable. Owners who live in urban areas may have no choice but to board their horses. Boarding stables fulfill a definite need for people who want to own and ride horses but do not have the facilities or property to keep them.

Boarding stables are usually a combination of housing facility and riding school. Typically, they include a large barn with box stalls, stalls with paddocks, an arena, schooling rings, tack room, and many large pastures. Most boarding operations employ a full-time barn manager and staff to care for the horses and the entire facility. Monthly boarding rates depend on how much care your horse needs, whether you want a private stall and paddock or an open turnout in group pastures, a particular type of grain and hay, and how many feedings you want per day. Some boarding stables include feed in their rates; others will allow you to supply your own feed for a lower cost. Don't forget to ask if both full-time care and part-time care are available and if the feed is included. For a reduced fee, some stables will do one feeding and have you do the other. A less expensive option is finding a boarding stable with a smaller staff, basic stalls, and pastures. In this case, the owner may do all the horsekeeping chores. Full-time care means the stable's staff handles all feedings, stall cleanings, and pasture turnout. Obviously, this is more expensive than part-time or minimal care. Some boarding stables will offer reduced or free boarding if you agree to work there part-time. It's important to understand that all boarding stables have their own specific philosophy on horse care, owner responsibility, and equitation. To prevent any future misunderstandings, choose a stable with ideas similar to your own. A good boarding facility will offer riding lessons for all levels and ages, and use excellent schooling horses. If you are considering boarding your horse, research the possibilities. Talk to other owners, speak to local horse clubs, and visit different stables before making a final decision. The barn manager should be willing to give you a tour, answer all your questions, and introduce you to current boarders for their opinions and feedback. Carefully review the boarding contract and any rules before signing. If you fall in love with the situation and the contract is fair, most stables will take a refundable deposit to hold a stall for you. If you're not sure what to ask the stable manager, the checklist below will help.

Questions for the boarding manager

After touring the boarding facility, ask to sit down with the manager or owner to go over your concerns and questions. The following questions may help you decide if this is the place for your horse:

Boarding arrangements

- What type of boarding arrangements are available: stall, stall and paddock, pasture, or all three? Do you have a choice of full care, part care, or owner care only?
- What are the monthly fees for all arrangements?

◆ What do the monthly fees for full care and part care include? Feedings? Stall cleanings? Handling back and forth from stall to paddock and vice versa?

◆ Is stall bedding included in the fees or must you provide it?

◆ Can you supplement some pasture time to stall boarding and not use a paddock?

◆ Do you have a choice on stalls and/or pastures?

Feeding

◆ Does the monthly fee include hay and feed? If not, is there an extra charge for it? Do you need to make your own feed arrangements?

◆ What types of hay and concentrates are available on the premises?

◆ Where is the feed stored? Can you bring your own storage materials?

Health and emergency care

◆ Do they have an equine veterinarian who makes regular barn calls and is available for emergencies?

◆ What procedures are followed in an emergency?

◆ In an emergency, will your horse be taken to the nearest equine clinic or hospital? Will you be contacted immediately?

◆ What are the health requirements for horses boarding at the facility? Does the facility require all vaccinations or allow optional ones (strangles, rabies)?

◆ How current must a Coggins test result be?

Miscellaneous issues

◆ Will you have access to and use of the tack room and/or storage room?

◆ What is the policy on using the schooling rings, round pens, hot walkers, and the arena?

◆ Is there a place for you to keep your trailer?

◆ Do they have accident and liability insurance in case of an accident? Is this noted in the boarding contract?

◆ Are on-staff riding instructors available? Can you hire a freelance instructor?

◆ Do they have a farrier who makes regularly scheduled visits every six to eight weeks?

◆ Do they require a deposit when you sign the contract?

◆ May you have a copy of the contract to review?

◆ How many weeks' notice must you give when you want to leave?

◆ How must you pay your board fees and when are they due? Are there late fees?

◆ How will they notify you about any changes at the facility, including fees?

◆ Will you have 24/7 access to your horse? Are there set visiting hours?

◆ What type of security system is in place?

◆ What are the usual on-site hours for the staff? Will someone always be available to check on the horses?

Consider the answers to these questions before you decide where to keep your horse. Don't sign a contract right away. Take the time to review the contract carefully so you know what you and your horse are getting into. Most stables are very willing to work with you on your concerns and requests. They, too, want what's best for your horse since your praise and recommendation might attract more boarders to the facility.

Chapter 2

The Daily Grind: Feeding Your Horse the Right Diet

I f you want to keep your horse in top condition, you'll need to pay attention to providing him with a well-balanced diet and adhering to strict management practices. Before deciding on the best diet for him, you must understand his nutritional needs. In order for his body to function properly, he requires specific quantities of water, minerals, protein, vitamins, fats, and carbohydrates on a daily basis. Diets lacking these nutrients can result in poor fertility, a compromised immune system, weight loss, and deficiencies in muscle and bone maintenance. Nutrients are found in quality roughage, grains, concentrates, and clean water sources. A horse that requires higher amounts of nutrients in his diet can get them through supplements.

Water

Equine nutritionists consider water to be the most essential nutrient in a horse's diet. The average horse requires a minimum of eight to ten gallons of clean, readily available water, whether out on pasture or in a stall. Increase your horse's water intake if he or she lives in a hot climate, is pregnant or nursing, or is undergoing intense exercising and training. You can estimate your horse's actual water intake by using the following formula: two to three pounds of water to every pound of dry feed. A horse weighing 1,100 pounds that eats twenty-seven pounds of roughage and grain per day should be drinking between seven and eleven gallons of water. Large amounts of water assist in digestion, circulation, and in regulating body temperature. Water helps prevent colic, muscle injuries, and dehydration. It promotes cell repair, proper gastrointestinal functions, and the removal of body waste.

The water must be free of bacteria, algae, and high levels of nitrates and pesticides. These can cause severe digestive problems. If your water comes from a natural source, test it every three to four months. Local agricultural agencies can also help you determine the quality of your water source through testing. If your water comes from the local reservoir or a private water company, request the most recent testing results. Often state or federal agencies conduct these tests.

Minerals

For your horse to have healthy bones and muscles, excellent nerve and metabolic functions, and normal enzyme activities, he must have regular access to digestible minerals. Most horses require 5 percent of their daily diet to contain inorganic minerals, such as calcium, phosphorus, potassium, and sodium chloride. Excellent-quality hays, grains, and pastures easily meet your horse's mineral requirements.

In equine nutrition, calcium and phosphorus are grouped together because of the strong effect they have on one another. Calcium, which is vital to bone growth and muscle development in foals, is found in high amounts in roughage. Phosphorus is critical to the breakdown of fats and proteins and is abundant in grains. Each of these minerals plays a significant role in your horse's diet, but ingesting more phosphorus than calcium over an extended period of time prevents calcium absorption. Lack or loss of calcium can lead to irregular bone growth, skeletal disfigurement, and malnutrition. A deficiency in phosphorus can be just as devastating, causing extreme bone disorders, such as rickets. Therefore, you must maintain a calcium to phosphorus ratio (Ca:P) of more calcium than phosphorus. The exact ratio depends on the developmental stage of the horse. An adult horse should be on a 2:1 ratio, and foals should be on a 1.4:1 ratio. The minimum ratio for all horses is 1:1 and should never fall below this.

All pastures and stalls must have a salt block so that your horse has unlimited access to replenish his body's salt content on a daily basis.

Sodium chloride (NaCl), or salt, which makes up between .5 percent and 1 percent of your horse's total diet, is the only mineral he actually craves enough to seek out. Because salt is imperative to the regulation of body fluids, the acid-base balance, and the maintenance of muscle tissue, your horse needs plenty of it every day. Because horses lose two to five ounces of sodium a day through sweating and urination, they must replace it quickly. A typical salt block or salt lick is easily accessible and composed of 98 to 99 percent sodium chloride. You can place salt blocks in a stall or out on a pasture. Since the constant licking of the block normally forms a depression, you'll know if your horse has been using it.

Protein

Without a regular source of protein, your horse's soft-tissue structures may be compromised, weakening his muscles and ligaments and deforming his hooves. In addition, he won't have the internal fuel to grow and stay active. Amino acids, approximately twenty-two of them, are known as the building blocks of protein. Ten of these amino acids are considered essential, meaning that your horse must get sufficient amounts of them in his diet. These include lysine, arginine, and valine. An imbalance in the amount of essential amino acids prevents your horse from synthesizing any protein matter, which can cause a reduction in body conditioning, restricted growth in foals, performance problems, and poor fetal development. Crude protein (CP) is the term used by equine nutritionists and feed producers to represent the requirements and quantities of accessible protein in a horse's diet. The amount of digestible crude protein in a feed or ration is measured in percentages. For example, a typical adult horse requires a diet of 10 percent crude protein to meet his protein requirements. Foals and pregnant mares have higher protein demands. Their diets should consist of 12 to 14 percent crude protein. Of course, the amount of crude protein should fit the horse's growth stage, age, and nutritional needs. Too much protein is not much of a concern, but it can cause older horses to be prone to kidney problems from straining to remove excess nitrogen in grains and concentrates. Protein deficiency is mostly a problem for young foals and weanlings, but it can contribute to skin and hoof problems in adult horses.

Vitamins

Vitamins are organic compounds found in small amounts in quality grasses and concentrates. Your horse needs vitamins to regulate his body functions. Vitamins also work as coenzymes, crucial components of an enzyme that activates internal systems. The vitamin requirements in a horse's feed vary, depending on his stage of development, age, overall health, and level of physical activity. Your horse requires two groups of vitamins in his diet: fat-soluble and water-soluble.

The fat-soluble vitamins include vitamin A, vitamin E, vitamin D, and vitamin K. Your horse absorbs these vitamins into his body through lipids (fats) and stores them within fat cells.

Vitamin A: Affects vision, reproduction, and bone growth. Deficiencies of vitamin A can result in blindness, infertility, and ataxia. The body converts green grass and forages into vitamin A in the intestinal tract.

Vitamin E: Acts as an antioxidant. It occurs in green forage and quality hay, but its actual dietary benefits are unknown. Some experts believe that it may improve fertility and, when combined with selenium, may help treat the effects of degenerative musculoskeletal disease found in foals and young horses. However, these claims are unsubstantiated. Poor feed storage and mold growth reduce the amount of vitamin E in the feed.

Vitamin D: Is not considered a required vitamin in your horse's diet. The body synthesizes Vitamin D when sunlight rays activate its conversion and absorption into the skin. Your horse should have a minimum of an hour in strong sunlight every day; he needs more time outside if it's overcast or cloudy.

Vitamin K: Is essential in the formation of blood clots. The body can synthesize this vitamin from green forage or with bacteria found naturally in your horse's large intestinal tract. A horse deficient in vitamin K often bleeds spontaneously because of insufficient clotting factors.

The water-soluble vitamin group includes vitamin C and the subgroup, B-complex vitamins (biotin, thiamin, and riboflavin). Most of these vitamins are found in green foodstuffs or are synthesized by microbes in the large intestine. The body cannot store this group of vitamins. Therefore, your horse needs them replaced daily. If he is feeding on green pastures or eating high-quality forages, he should be able to replenish water-soluble vitamins.

Vitamin C: Assists in the production of hormones, nerve tissue, and skin collagen. It is found abundantly in fresh grass and is synthesized through the liver.

B-complex vitamins: Are associated with the metabolic transfer of energy. They are synthesized by bacteria in the large intestine (except B-12). Racehorses have a tendency to become deficient in B-complex vitamins and can become "track sour," a condition that results in a decreased appetite.

Fats and oils

Fats and oils are the most concentrated sources of dietary energy stored within your horse's body. Performance horses require higher levels of fat to increase usable energy levels and to improve the storage of glycogen, a reserve supply of energy. For the pregnant mare and athletic horse, fats and oils should make up at least 10 percent of their total diet. Vegetable oil, commercial feeds, and nutritional supplements are sources of dietary fats. Your horse needs the right amount of fats in his diet to suit his age, workload, and lifestyle. If his diet is too rich in fats and his exercise level is too low to burn the calories, he could gain a great deal of weight, begin displaying stable vices, and possibly develop laminitis. Know your horse's energy requirements and the exact amount of fats and oils included in his diet to ensure that he is in optimal condition. Store all feed that contains high levels of fat or pure fat and oil sources in airtight containers or feed bins. Prolonged exposure to air causes fats and oils to become rancid and eventually ruins your feed.

Carbohydrates

Horses obtain their primary source of energy from carbohydrates. Because carbohydrates make up 50 to 80 percent of plant matter, this nutrient is the principal component of your horse's diet. Carbohydrates in soluble or fiber form are digested in the small intestine and stomach. During this process, carbohydrates are synthesized into volatile fatty acids to be converted into energy and fermented gases. Your horse's muscles and liver are able to store carbohydrates as glycogen; this is energy on reserve, waiting to be released during intense exercise. Most horses receive an adequate level of carbohydrates from green grasses. For higher energy needs, you'll have to feed grains such as oats and barley, which are rich in carbohydrates.

Roughage

Roughage includes legumes and grasses in dried or fresh form. Horses demand daily amounts of roughage or forage as their primary source of minerals, carbohydrates, protein, and fiber to meet their nutritional requirements and to maintain a healthy digestive system. Although roughage provides less energy, it does supply sufficient amounts of calcium and vitamin A. Of course to have any dietary value, forages must always be high quality and properly processed. Eating roughage forces your horse to chew, producing enzymes in his saliva that aid and improve digestion. This is extremely important since poor digestion can lead to a severe case of colic.

Coastal hay.

Types of roughage

Grasses, either dried or fresh from a pasture, are the most common forage. They are an excellent source of protein, fiber, and vitamins. Although grasses do not provide much energy, they are easy to digest. They are classified as cool season or warm season. Cool-season grasses are at their best between early fall and early spring; warm-season grasses reach their peak during the late spring and throughout the summer. Ryegrass, tall wheatgrass and fescue are categorized as cool-season forages. They are higher in quality, richer in protein, and typically more palatable than warm-season grasses. The warm-season grasses, such as Bahia, Bermuda, coastal, and Johnson, are suitable sources of fiber but low in nutritional value. Hay should be cut every four to six weeks during a dry period and baled for storage. Although you can use it for up to a year, it is best when used within six months of being baled so that it retains its dietary value, digestibility, and flavor.

Fresh grass is the best source of roughage you can feed your horse because it keeps its high nutritional value. A strict pasture management program that includes regular and consistent fertilization, rotation, raking, and inspections ensures the health and viability of your pastures. Of course, the dietary value of pasture grass varies slightly with the seasons (especially winter), but most adult pleasure horses can meet all their roughage requirements from grazing solely on pasture grass.

Legumes, the other class of roughage loved by horses, include

Alfalfa pellets.   **Alfalfa hay.**

alfalfa and clover. These differ from grass in that they have longer stems and rounder leaves. They are included in the cool-season forage group. Of the two, alfalfa is more popular with horse owners and safer to feed. Alfalfa is a good source of energy and is rich in minerals, protein, and vitamin A. Since alfalfa also has a high level of calcium (the Ca:P ratio is 6:1), you must make sure to balance it out with a grain (phosphorus source) when you formulate your horse's diet. Alfalfa comes as long-stem hay, either processed into cubes or pellets or chopped and dried. The pellet and cube forms are much easier for your horse to digest, extremely flavorsome, and free of blister beetles and weeds. Because alfalfa is so rich in nutrients, it costs slightly more than basic hay, especially if it has been processed.

Clover is a less common type of legume that comes in varieties, such as red and sweet clover. Although similar to alfalfa in palatability, clover does not have the same nutritional benefits. If it is moldy, sweet clover can be highly toxic and even deadly. To avoid this risk, most owners do not feed their horses clover and don't allow them to graze on pastures containing it.

Quality of harvested roughage

Excellent quality and careful selection of harvested roughage are important when buying and choosing hay. Consider the following when making any decisions concerning your roughage source.

Type of forage: Determine whether the cool-season or the warm-season variety is obtainable locally and which is best for your horse's dietary needs.

Age of grass: Grasses cut at early growth stages contain more nutrients. As grasses mature, their nutritional values decrease, but their fiber content increases. Do not use hay that is more than a year old.

Appearance: The grass should be leafy and greenish in color, indicating high levels of vitamins. It should not have too many long stems, and it should be free of weeds. Hay should also be free of dirt, garbage, mold, and insects.

Odor: Take a good whiff. If you smell anything moldy, pungent, or musty, avoid it. The odor should be fresh and sweet.

Daily roughage requirements

Hay and grasses can make up to half of an active adult horse's daily feeding. For a horse that isn't active or for an older horse, high-quality hay and grass can meet all of his daily roughage requirements. As a general rule, horses that are full-time grazers should eat 1.5 to 2 percent of their total body weight a day in forages. Horses with limited or no access to grazing must have at least 1 percent of their total body weight a day in forages. Athletic horses need to eat 2 to 3 percent of their total body weight in forages to meet their daily requirements. Remember, these are just basic guidelines to consider when creating the right ration for your horse. In equine nutrition, the standard is that all horses must eat at least 1 percent of their body weight as forage. Therefore, a horse weighing one thousand pounds requires a minimum of ten pounds of roughage per day. Falling below this could lead to colic, weight loss, nutritional deficiencies and disorders, and diminished mental ability. When formulating your horse's ration, fulfill his roughage requirements first, then supplement with pure grains or concentrates for balance.

Concentrates

Concentrates are pure or mixed grains in natural or processed forms. They are a major source of vitamins, minerals, and carbohydrates. Owners give concentrates to active horses because they are an excellent source of energy and minerals. Concentrates, typically low in fiber and calcium, need to be combined with roughage and supplements. Grains come rolled, flaked, or in pellet form (which makes them more digestible). These forms are cost efficient, lengthen their shelf life, and help maintain nutrients as well as allow for easier storage. Most horse owners purchase well-balanced concentrates produced by large feed companies and local feed cooperatives. The typical grains in a horse's

Flaked corn.

diet are oats, corn, and barley. They can be fed alone or blended with other grains; commercial feeds also have them in various proportions.

Corn

Of all the grains, corn has the highest energy content. Because it's high in carbohydrates and low in fiber and protein, be careful when including it in your horse's diet. Balance it with either oats or good-quality hay. Many owners feed oats and corn in equal portions to guarantee that their horses are getting a ration filled with both energy and fiber. Since it is a major source of dietary energy and fats, corn is primarily fed to active and high-performance horses that undergo daily exercise and intensive training. Corn is also beneficial for putting weight on young and underweight horses as part of a consistent feeding program.

In addition to whole corn, there are many different types of corn that you can feed horses. Rolled, cracked, and flaked corn are easy to digest. Do not feed cornmeal to horses since it requires very little chewing and is not easily digestible, which may cause a bad case of colic. The only true drawback in feeding processed corn is its lower energy value, making it less potent than whole corn. For a high-energy diet, feed whole corn as loose kernels or straight off the cob. Always check the corn for mold before feeding. Eating large amounts of moldy corn can cause a horse to become extremely sick; some horses die within a day or two of eating it.

Oats

Oats are the most popular feed grain because they are safe, tasty, and full of fiber. Even if a horse is overfed oats, his chances of developing colic or another digestive problem are very low. On the other hand, oats cost more than other grains, are not exceptionally nutritious, and are a poor source of energy. Oats do have a high amount of protein; however, you can get protein from other sources at much lower prices. On the other hand, the fact that oats are a low-risk, very tasty, bulky feed makes them worth every penny to some owners. Most horses can comfortably digest both whole and processed oats, which usually come in crimped or rolled form. Because processed oats are easy to chew and digest, they are an ideal feed for yearlings and older horses. Store oats carefully to avoid excessive moisture and dust buildup, which can lead to nutrient loss and rapid spoilage.

Barley

Although not always found in feed stores, barley is an excellent grain to include in a high-energy diet, and it is a good source of protein. In most equine diets, barley is not the main ingredient; usually, you mix it with a high-fiber grain, such as oats or wheat bran. Avoid using crushed barley; feed only flaked or rolled types. As with corn, be careful about how much barley your horse eats daily and avoid any quick increases or decreases in amounts.

Sweet feeds

Horses are highly selective and ruled by their taste buds when it comes to what they like to eat. The delicious taste of molasses in sweet feed makes it a particular favorite. Commercially blended feeds that combine grains and molasses are rich in protein, vitamins, and minerals. They are carefully formulated to meet the elevated energy requirements of growing horses, lactating mares, and active horses. You can use pure molasses as an inexpensive feed additive for better flavoring

Oats.

Cream barley.

Sweet feed.

and to reduce the dust factor associated with many dry concentrates. Whether in sweet feed or used as a "top-dresser" on other feeds, molasses should only make up between 6 and 10 percent of your horse's daily diet. As with any grain, complement it with excellent-quality roughage.

Selecting the right concentrate

If you're able to blend grains together to create a balanced ration for your horse that meets all his nutritional and energy requirements, be very, very proud of yourself. Through trial and error, some owners have learned what grains work for their horses, how much of each is needed, and what proportion of forage is best. Most owners, however, lack the experience, knowledge, and confidence to mix grains on their own or to decide which are best for their horses.

Commercial feed companies produce safe and nutritional concentrates that remove some of the worry and nutritional guesswork about grains. That doesn't mean an owner shouldn't have some knowledge about feeds and feeding. Every owner needs to know how much to feed, why it's important to use a particular feed, and what the feed is doing or not doing nutritionally. Interpreting the feed tag on a sack of concentrates could be the subject of an entire book; it involves a real science lesson. However, simply knowing how much energy the feed provides and the best way to balance it with a horse's forage intake is the goal here. A feed tag shows percentages of crude protein and crude fiber. The lower the percentage of crude fiber, the higher the amount of energy the feed contains. Concentrates for an active horse should not have more than 9 to 10 percent crude fiber and should contain from 12 to 14 percent crude protein. This is a general guideline, something to keep in mind when deciding which concentrate meets your horse's needs. Before putting your horse on a new or different concentrate, consult your veterinarian, especially if you have questions or concerns.

If you've decided to put your horse on a commercial concentrate or to change to another one, keep these suggestions in mind:

♦ Visit your local feed store and speak to the staff about a feeding program for your horse. Be prepared to tell them his age, activity level, and approximate weight. Find out what brands and types of horse feeds they carry. Ask for a price list and about any discounts they may offer.

♦ Write down the crude protein and crude fiber contents and ingredients from the feeds you're considering. Before changing over to a new feed, compare the new feed to the current one.

Surprisingly, they may be the same or very similar.

◆ Ask for a brochure on the feeds you're considering. The information provided gives you an overview of the feed content, nutritional values, and feeding directions. Some feed stores may even give you a free sample to try. Visit the website of the commercial producers for additional information.

◆ Talk to your veterinarian about the feeds you are interested in, including the nutritional information on each and why you want to make the switch.

Mixed grain pellets.

Feeding concentrates

When feeding concentrates, keep in mind that they should meet all your horse's work and activity demands and enhance his conditioning and performance. You must balance all types of grain rations with the daily intake of roughage, and you should have the correct protein level to suit the developmental stage of your horse. As a general rule, a typical adult horse should eat a minimum of .75 percent of his total body weight in concentrates and mixed grains. For example, a horse that weighs one thousand pounds should have a minimum of 7.5 pounds of concentrate in his daily diet (1,000-pound horse x .75 percent = 7.5 pounds). The amount and type of concentrate changes based on your horse's age and activity level. Young horses up to yearling age should be fed 1 to 3 percent of their total body weight in high-protein concentrates to build healthy muscles and bones. Performance horses require from 1 to 2.5 percent of their total body weight in high-energy concentrates to increase their stamina and fuel their engines. One of the most important things to remember when feeding concentrates is to give them at regular times. It is much easier and safer for horses to eat concentrates twice a day at least twelve hours apart. Many owners find that feedings at 7:00 a.m. and 7:00 p.m. fit their schedules and satisfy their horse's hunger. Horses training intensely or performing on the show circuit can eat concentrates three times a day or every eight hours. Increasing the number of feedings doesn't mean increasing the amount of feed. Divide the required daily amount of concentrates equally among the feedings.

Nutritional supplements

If your horse needs additional nutrients, you can use several types of supplements to balance his diet. Supplements that offer more protein, minerals, vitamins, fat, and electrolytes are available. Nutritional supplements seem to benefit horses that have heavy workloads, suffer from poor hoof quality and hoof disorders, have weight-gain problems, infertility issues, or are pregnant or lactating. Although supplements have been available for years through veterinarians, they have skyrocketed in popularity due to endorsements from top trainers and professional competitors. Horse owners read advertisements about the enhanced body conditioning and stamina of athletic horses on supplements and want the same benefits for their horse, but the results are not always the same.

Most commercial supplements correct a specific condition or serve a specific purpose. However, some are more general and offer a variety of minerals, vitamins, amino acids, and electrolytes in one complete mixture. Commercially produced supplements are not cheap. In fact,

Nutritional supplements can be an excellent addition to your horse's daily diet. Always follow the suggested dosage and let your veterinarian know what types of supplements you're using.

the more specialized they are, the more expensive they tend to be. You can add basic supplements like vegetable oil, fish oil, and molasses to your horse's diet to increase fats and vitamins and to boost his energy level. Because a high-energy diet is often low in protein, you may need to supplement it with soybean meal, linseed meal, and cottonseed meal. Salt is the only required supplement all horses must have free access to, and salt blocks are inexpensive and available at most feed stores.

Remember that you don't have to put your horse on nutritional supplements. As previously noted, a typical adult horse meets all his nutritional needs by feeding on good-quality hay and concentrates. Unless your horse has greatly increased his energy level, is eating poor-quality forage, or has a known nutrient deficiency, buying supplements is a waste of money. Be sure to speak to your veterinarian or farrier before putting your horse on any type of supplement.

Creating a feeding management program

To be sure your horse is getting all his nutrients, formulate a well-balanced ration consisting of roughage, concentrates, or both. Base this on his total body weight and activity level. Growing horses and pregnant or lactating mares may require higher or lower amounts of roughage and concentrates. First, you must determine basic feeding guidelines based on body weight alone, and then compare that to roughage to concentrate ratios. Again, always consult your veterinarian to help you develop the best diet for your horse.

Feeding guidelines by body weight percentages

If not grazing on pasture: From 1 to 2 percent of his body weight per day in roughage. Do not allow him to fall below .75 percent of his body weight per day.

1,000-pound horse x 1 percent = 10 pounds of good-quality harvested roughage

If grazing on pasture: From 1 to 3 percent of his body weight in roughage per day.

1,000-pound horse x 1 percent = 10 pounds of good-quality pasture roughage

Feeding a concentrate for additional energy: From .75 to 1.5 percent of his body weight in concentrate. Do not allow him to fall below .75 percent of his body weight per day.

1,000-pound horse x 1 percent = 10 pounds of concentrate

Total daily intake of roughage and concentrate: From 1.5 to 3 percent of his body weight. The average total intake is 2 percent of total body weight.

1,000-pound horse x 2 percent = 20 pounds of concentrate/roughage

Feeding for energy: roughage to concentrate ratio

You cannot base a sensible diet solely on body weight percentages; they are just part of the information you need to create a diet that satisfies all of your horse's nutritional needs. Intensive competitions and training are important considerations when determining the correct proportion of roughage to concentrates for his ration. Equine nutritionists suggest using these established ratios, based on activity and workload:

No activity: Horses on pasture full-time; ridden only once or twice a week.

100 percent roughage

Light activity: Walking and some trotting up to two hours a day; ridden three to five times a week.

75 to 85 percent roughage/25 to 15 percent concentrates

Moderate activity: Walking, trotting, cantering, and galloping from two to three hours daily; ridden every day; training for hunter-jumper, cross-country eventing, reining, and driving.

60 to 70 percent roughage/40 to 30 percent concentrates

Heavy activity: Engaged in racing, polo, grand-prix level competitions, and endurance riding; hard galloping for long distances; daily training sessions of three hours or more.

50 percent roughage/50 percent concentrates

To guarantee a successful feeding management program, keep these additional criteria in mind:

- ◆ Your horse should have free access to eight to twelve gallons of clean water per day, more if he is in training or if you have a pregnant or lactating mare.
- ◆ Salt blocks must always be available in stalls and pastures.
- ◆ Establish regular feedings with equal time between them, two or three times a day.
- ◆ Never feed old, dirty, or indigestible feeds.

◆ Stall-kept horses should be fed hay in a rack or hay net, never on the floor.

◆ When making changes in your horse's diet, do so over time and not hastily. Sudden changes may cause colic or laminitis.

Determining a horse's weight

Since your horse's diet is partially based on his body weight, you need to know what that weight is. Fortunately, you don't need a livestock scale, which is expensive and usually found only at veterinary clinics or racing barns. You can measure your horse's girth with a cloth tape measure and then apply the number of inches to a standard formula (see below), or you can use a height and weight tape that gives a weight reading in pounds.

Here's what you do:

◆ Have someone hold your horse still while you measure him. Stand by your horse's left shoulder and take about two steps back, until you are behind his elbow.

◆ Place one end of the tape on his right side at his withers. Hold it in place with your right thumb and let it fall. You could also have a helper hold it in place and carefully pass the other end of the tape to you underneath the horse's barrel.

◆ Bend down slightly and use your left hand to reach for the tape.

◆ While holding both ends of the tape, center it to make sure it's positioned well behind the horse's elbow, around where the girth or cinch would go, or slightly farther back.

◆ Make sure you have the top of the tape correctly positioned on the right side of his withers. Then, match up the ends. Where they meet gives you either the total number of inches of the heart-girth (HG) with a measuring tape or the total weight in pounds using a height and weight tape.

◆ If you are using the formula method, you'll need to know his body length. Measure from the point of the shoulder to the farthest point on his buttocks. This gives you his body length (BL) in inches.

◆ Put the measurements you've taken into this formula:

$$\text{Weight} = \text{heartgirth}^2 \text{ (in inches)} \times \text{body length (in inches)} \div 330$$

or

$$\text{Weight} = \frac{HG^2 \times BL}{330}$$

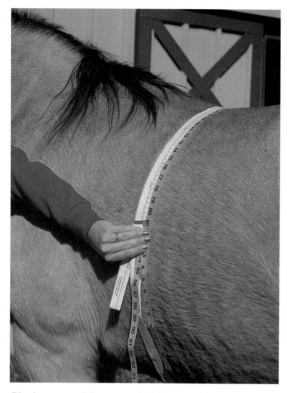

Placing a weight tape (white tape) around your horse's girth will give you his weight. A measuring tape (yellow tape) will give you his heartgirth in inches.

This should give you an estimated weight, within eighty to one hundred pounds of your horse's actual weight. If it seems off or too high from the last time he was weighed, take the measurements again using a height and weight tape. If the weight reading is still way off, call your veterinarian so he or she can determine the reason for the discrepancy.

Traits of a good diet

With a wide variety of feeds available, it's becoming easier to choose the right diet for your horse. Grain and concentrate manufacturers produce quality feeds that meet certain standards. Because the number of forage producers has increased, growing high-quality hay and selling it at affordable prices is the only way for these producers to stay in business. As more research is done in equine nutrition, manufacturers produce and sell more nutritious and high-quality feeds. Before you make the final decision on what to feed your horse, you should take into account the following factors. Ask if the feed is:

Safe: The concentrate or forage must be free from dust or mold. Smell the hay for any unusual odors and look for any insects or weeds. Look through a sample bale and find out what type of forage it is. You don't want a species prone to toxicity problems. If the hay bale seems too dry, lacks color, or is full of stems, it could cause colic.

Palatable: If it doesn't taste good, your horse won't eat it. Manufacturers process commercial feeds with taste in mind. Hays and legumes should be leafy to meet nutritional needs but also because that's where the flavor is. Stems are not very palatable or nutritious, just added bulk. If possible, ask to try a sample of hay or concentrate before investing in something your horse refuses eat.

Economical: The price of feed varies, depending on the type of concentrate and forage, energy levels, ingredients, weight, commercial brand, location, and whether it is processed or unprocessed. The feed should meet all of your horse's nutritional and energy requirements at a price that is affordable. Concentrates are more expensive than forages. Determine whether or not your horse really needs concentrates because if he doesn't need them, you're wasting money. Just because one brand is cheaper than another doesn't mean the second brand is not a quality feed. Compare the feed tags and look for the differences. Make sure your horse likes the feed before buying too much of it; opened feed is usually not returnable.

Processing and packaging: Buying commercial concentrates guarantees high-quality blends of grain processed under strict guidelines and in clean environments. Grains and processed forages are packaged in strong, water-resistant sacks that are easy to store and that prevent excessive moisture, heat damage, and mold contamination. Roughage bales should be bound by wire or bale strings, free of any foreign objects, and tagged with the forage type and the harvest date.

Nutritious: This is probably the most important factor. The ration should be full of minerals, proteins, fats, and vitamins and should be a good source of fiber. The diet should be balanced, digestible, rich in nutrients, and satisfy all of your horse's nutritional demands.

Feeding methods

Feeding concentrates

Once you've figured out what to feed your horse, you should decide how you're going to feed him. Choose a method that best suits his living space and diet content. You should feed most horses individually since each horse has different dietary needs. Don't feed concentrates the same

Use a measuring scoop to weigh your horse's concentrate portion carefully. You need to give him the exact amount for each feeding. Do not casually add or decrease the amount of concentrate or guess how much to give.

way you feed forages. Scoop concentrates out of their storage bins with a feed scoop at a set measurement, such as a two-quart scoop (a full scoop is equal to two quarts of grain). The expensive scale-scoop is a brilliant combination of weighing scale and feed scoop. When you put feed into the scale-scoop, the dial moves to indicate the exact weight of the grain in pounds. Never use a coffee can or plastic milk jug to measure the amount of grain and don't rely on guesses based on eyeballing it. Always weigh the concentrates using a measured feed scoop or kitchen scale.

The best way to feed concentrates is from a flat-back plastic bucket, a rubber feed pan, or a mountable plastic feeder. Sizes range from a one-gallon stall feeder to a four-gallon rubber pan to a mountable pasture feeder that holds twenty-two gallons. The most commonly used feeder holds four to six gallons, which is more than sufficient for the pastured and stabled horse that is fed at least twice daily.

If your horse lives out on pasture and needs to be fed concentrates, fill a bucket or rubber feed pan with his feed and place it on the ground. Stay around to make sure other horses in the pasture aren't eyeing his feed. If necessary, take him to an area free of other horses to allow him to eat undisturbed. Never dump the concentrate directly onto the ground. You'll risk the possibility that he'll also eat manure and dirt along with it and spread the feed around so much that he doesn't eat the full amount.

A stabled horse should have his concentrates fed to him either in a mounted corner feeder or in a flat-back bucket hung on the wall at eye level. Many owners prefer plain flat-back buckets to permanent wall feeders since they can be removed and not left to be cribbed and chewed on. Owners also use rubber feed pans in stall feedings, but they are not as popular since your horse can easily knock them over, step on them, and pick them up.

Feeding forages

You can feed regular hay and unprocessed alfalfa in hay racks and nets in stalls. You can put them into large pasture feeders or set them up as hay rolls and stacks. For a stabled horse, weigh processed and unprocessed forages to guarantee that your horse is getting the correct amounts. Hay flakes separate very easily. You can weigh them using a hanging scale or large kitchen scale with at least a ten-pound capacity. Just as feeding hay becomes a repetitive routine, sometimes the measuring does, too. For instance, owners who consistently weigh forages start to notice a pattern in their horse's eating. He may be eating three flakes at each feeding. Unfortunately, this pattern often tempts owners to stop weighing the forages and just grab three flakes. Hay and alfalfa bales vary in size, and no two are ever exactly alike. Even hay bales from the same producer can vary tremendously in weight from one batch to the next. That's why you really should weigh the flakes; those few extra minutes to get an exact weight could actually prevent a bout of colic or laminitis.

After weighing the flakes, place them either in a hay rack or hay net. A hay rack is a permanent, wall-mounted fixture designed to be wider at the top to accommodate large amounts of hay. The slanted shape and thin bars allow the horse to eat the loose hay protruding through the open spaces. Place the hay rack at a level that does not strain your horse to reach it, but not so low that he could injure himself on it. The fact that you can't move the hay rack around or adjust the height is a major drawback, leading most owners to opt for the portable and adjustable hay net or hay bag.

A hay net is a large bag made of knotted nylon or cotton cord that can hold twenty-five to thirty pounds of hay. Because it is constructed of gathering rings and strong nylon cord, you can safely tie it to a stall door or wall. A hay net is more useful for temporary feedings and is perfect for shows or trailers. Once your horse has eaten all his hay, promptly

Hay nets are a good way to feed hay in a stall, on a trailer, or at a show. Because you should not feed hay on the ground, hay nets and hay bags allow you to feet hay cleanly, safely, and conveniently.

remove the hay net, otherwise it could become a great chewing toy. If it is worn down enough, it falls apart, making it very easy for your horse to choke on it. To get your horse to eat his hay more slowly, buy a hay net with smaller openings or consider using a hay bag instead. A hay bag is also a helpful feeding tool for horses that tend to gorge their hay or are overweight and on a controlled diet. Hay bags serve the same purpose as hay nets, but they are designed slightly differently. They are made of a solid material, such as canvas or vinyl, and have only a small opening in the front. The horse pulls the hay from this front opening. Nylon straps hold the bag up, and reinforced seams hold the hay tightly inside. Many owners prefer hay bags since they are made of waterproof material, have one small opening, and are easier to stuff with hay and to secure in place. Hay bags offer better protection from water, a reduced loss of hay, and convenience.

Usually, pasture horses do not need supplements with any hay or alfalfa unless the quality of the grass is poor or can't sustain the horse's nutritional needs. For a hay-deficient pasture, hay rolls and hay stacks are good options. You can set up several large feeders or tire feeders around the pasture to give horses free access to the hay. Horses fed exclusively on pasture grass can receive hay supplements during the winter months.

Group feeding

Group feeding is common on large breeding and training farms that have many horses at the same developmental stage or on identical diets. For example, you could group feed young horses under two years old, broodmares, and performance horses undergoing the same intensive training regimen. Group feeding is definitely more convenient for an owner than individual feeding, but it has several disadvantages. Aggressive horses keep the timid ones from getting access to feed by kicking or scaring them off. Some horses can overeat while others go completely unfed. Hungry horses may start feed bolting in a desperate attempt to get their share during the feeding frenzy. With all the feed divided among several large feeders, you have a difficult time gauging how much each horse is actually eating. To ease the mad dash to the feed, spread several feeders around the pasture to help spread out the horses. The only time that group feeding is really necessary is for foals.

Creep feeding

At about two months of age, foals need more protein and energy than their mother's milk can provide them. You can feed foals 1 percent of their body weight in concentrates per day. Creep feeding is the best way for foals to have safe access to feed. It prevents hungry mares from eating any additional feed. A "creep" feeder is so named because the foal literally has to creep through a small opening or under low bars to get into the feeder. The box-shaped feeder with bars or panels on four sides is usually large enough to hold up to three foals. It provides just enough space on the bottom for foals to get in and out of it easily, and it is completely mare-proof. Place creep feeders close to where your mares primarily graze to encourage their foals to enter and use it. Check feeders daily for dirt, remaining feed, and weathering. Since the feeder is easily accessible, foals should have no problem getting to eat sometime throughout the day. For the first week, inspect the feeder several times a day to assess how much feed the foals are eating. One or two foals might be consuming too much feed and not leaving enough for the other foals. Aggressive or constantly hungry foals may need to be fed separately. Creep-feed rations generally should be high in crude protein with a 1.6:1 calcium:phosphorus ratio. Several high-quality commercial concentrates specially formulated for foals and weanlings are available. For the most part, creep feeding benefits your foal's feeding program and weaning experience. You can purchase a basic creep feeder from a local feed store or by mail order.

Body condition scoring system

The system devised for scoring body condition (see Appendix 3) was originally used to determine the reproductive abilities of a mare based on her body fat and where the fat is deposited. Using scores and descriptions set by researchers, with 1 representing the poorest condition and 9 identifying extremes in fat, owners can rate their mares and decide whether or not they are fit for breeding. Mares must have a score of 6 or 7 to be considered for breeding. Studies have shown that mares with a score of less than 5, or "moderate," are not as fertile as mares scoring 6 or 7, and they have fewer heat cycles. They also experience difficulties with a full-term pregnancy and have lactation problems.

Recently, some owners have applied the body-condition scoring system to assess the health and conditioning of all horses. Some trainers use the system to predict the athletic ability of young horses and to troubleshoot potential health problems. Body condition scores are open to interpretation since horse breeds vary in muscling, height, and the

According to the Body Condition Scoring System, this horse scores between 8 (fat) and 9 (extremely fat). Ideally, mares should score between 5 and 7 to be considered fit for breeding.

amount of fat. If you want to use the body score system for other than breeding purposes, take the score descriptions and compare them to your breed's standard. For a Quarter Horse, the score of moderate to fleshy may describe ideal conditioning, whereas for an Arabian, the score of moderately thin is the desired body type. In general, most breeds fall between scores of 4 and 7, with 5 considered the ideal score. When considering whether or not to breed your mare, use the exact body-condition score descriptions to determine if you should breed her.

Poisonous plants and trees

Lurking within our pastures are numerous varieties of poisonous plants that can cause severe health problems, intense reactions, and even death if ingested. Among the plants classified as poisonous are certain kinds of weeds, wildflowers, shrubs, herbs, and trees. Within each of these groups, some species are absolutely deadly to horses and other livestock. The levels of toxicity in these plants are categorized from low to very high, causing general or specific health disorders. You can purchase field guides that illustrate and describe in detail common poisonous plants. These books offer information about toxicity levels, geographical locations, and general reactions when ingested. Use one of these books when inspecting your pastures. Conduct this inspection on a weekly basis. Local agricultural agencies also have free literature and reference materials to help you identify poisonous plants indigenous to your region. You must set aside time to ensure that pastures are safe and free from all poisonous plants. Use preventative measures, such as spraying herbicides, mowing, and tree pruning, regularly. Don't believe the fallacy that horses can distinguish between a safe and unsafe plant simply by smell. You don't want to lose your horse to something that is easily preventable. That would be a tragedy.

The poisonous plants discussed below are some of the most toxic. They pose an immediate threat to your horse's health. Consult a field guide or your local agricultural agency to learn about toxic plants common to your area.

Showy milkweed (*Asclepias speciosa*).

Milkweed *(Asclepias spp)*: This weed is found all over North America. The deadly toxin occurs in different concentrations, depending on the species of milkweed. Signs of poisoning include respiratory difficulties, unsteadiness, colic, and heart-rate irregularities. They are noticeable within twelve hours of consumption. Treatment is possible if you detect the signs early and if your horse has not eaten too much of the milkweed.

Oleander *(Nerium oleander)* Highly poisonous, this ornamental and flowering shrub grows throughout the southeastern and southwestern United

Oleander (*Nerium oleander*).

Japanese yew leaves (*Taxus japonicus*) and fruits.

Water hemlock (*Cicuta douglasii*).

States. Deadly even in small amounts, it can kill a horse within a few hours of eating it. Typical signs of oleander poisoning are severe colic, diarrhea, and cardiac and respiratory irregularities.

Yew *(Taxius spp):* The yew family includes trees and shrubs found throughout North America. Different yews have different toxins, collectively called taxine. Death can be immediate for horses that ingest too much of it. Clinical signs of yew poisoning are muscle tremors, convulsions, diarrhea, and respiratory problems. Never plant these shrubs where your horse might have access to them.

Water hemlock *(Cicuta spp):* Also known as the muskrat weed, water hemlock is highly toxic. Several species grow throughout North America in wet grasslands, riverbanks, and in other types of wetlands. Water hemlock contains the deadly neurotoxin cicutoxin, which causes noticeable tremors and seizures, respiratory difficulties, and an accelerated heart rate. Death is almost always inevitable; some horses die within three hours of ingesting a deadly dosage.

Red maple *(Acer rubrum):* Although this tree produces beautiful foliage in the fall, the dried and wilted leaves are the source of its deadly toxin. Young green leaves are not a threat. Eating the aged leaves and bark, which contains the toxin, severely damages the structure of a horse's red blood cells. The result is anemia, rapid heart and breathing rates, discoloration

Red maple tree (*Acer rubrum*).

of the urine, and death. Treatment of red maple poisoning with high doses of vitamin C and I.V. fluids has met with some success; but there is no guarantee, and symptoms must be detected in the earliest stages. Never plant red maples close to barns or allow them to remain in pastures. Remove fallen branches immediately and always make sure wood shavings for bedding are not from red maple trees.

Common forage disorders

Forage poisoning is a common cause of death in horses since most owners don't expect it and aren't on the lookout for any potential dangers. The sad reality is that most of these disorders are preventable using good pasture management and careful selection of harvested forages. Consult with local agricultural agents about forage toxicity issues in your area; be sure you purchase all baled or rolled forages from a respected and experienced producer.

Sorghum toxicity

The forage family of sorghums includes Sudan grass (*Sorghum vulgare*), Johnsongrass (*Sorghum halapense*), and certain sorghum hybrids. This family contains prussic acid. Fast periods of growth after mowing or a drought can cause the prussic acid to be converted into lethal cyanide. Cyanide poisoning can be deadly to a horse that consumes large amounts of tainted sorghum. Common signs of cyanide poisoning over time include labored breathing, colic, urinary problems, and cystitis. To prevent problems, monitor pastures of sorghum forages during their growth stages. Only allow horses onto them once the grass has reached a height of eighteen to twenty inches. Never let your horse graze on newly growing sorghum pastures. Some cyanide-free species of hybrid sorghums are available. These are safer alternatives to natural species of Sudan and Johnsongrass.

Fescue-grass poisoning

In general, fescue grass is not a serious threat to most horses, but it can cause complications in pregnant mares. The source of the danger is a fungus commonly found in the fescue seeds. Broodmares who eat large amounts of fescue during the last few weeks of their pregnancy are prone to thick placentas and to extended gestation periods, which may result in foaling difficulties and in foal mortality.

Blister beetles

Blister beetles cause painful blisters when they land on your skin and release their defensive toxin, known as cantharidin. They often swarm around alfalfa fields to feed and reproduce. When alfalfa is harvested, the blister beetles are crushed and trapped within the bale. The remains of the dead beetles in the baled alfalfa contain cantharidin. When ingested, this is highly toxic, even in minimal amounts. The first sign of blister-beetle poisoning is usually colic, but as the digestive system absorbs the toxin, discolored urine and constant convulsions can occur. If you catch the poisoning soon enough, the horse may recover. However, this poison is hard to diagnose and difficult to treat. The best way to prevent blister-beetle poisoning is to buy alfalfa from experienced producers who use special equipment that removes dead beetles, whole and crushed, prior to baling and who inspect sample bales for possible blister-beetle contamination. Many veterinarians recommend feeding horses processed and not harvested alfalfa to avoid the threat of blister beetles.

Sweet-clover toxicity

Sweet clover is a common legume that thrives across North American pastures and roadsides. When it becomes moldy, the fungi living on it produce a toxin known as dicoumarin, which interferes with the body's ability to form blood clots. When blood can't coagulate, constant nosebleeds and internal hemorrhaging may occur. Unlike other types of poisoning, sweet-clover toxicity usually builds up over time and rarely causes immediate death. Signs of poisoning from sweet clover can take up to three weeks to be noticed. Besides being weak and depressed, horses have excessive swellings, nosebleeds, cuts that don't stop bleeding,

Yellow sweet clover (*Melilotus officinalis*).

anemia, and lameness. Treatments typically consist of blood transfusions and a series of vitamin K shots. As with other instances of forage and plant poisoning, early detection is critical to your horse's survival. Because mold is the catalyst that changes sweet clover from safe to deadly, you must inspect it carefully. A reliable producer properly cures all harvested clover. Since it can take time for any symptoms to be noticed, as a precaution, do not feed pregnant mares or horses undergoing a scheduled surgery or procedure any type of sweet clover for at least three weeks prior to their due date or surgery date.

Helpful feeding hints

Even if your horse is on the best-formulated diet, which means that all his dietary needs are being met, you won't be helping him if you don't have a consistent feeding routine in place. How and when you feed is just as important as what you feed. Consult your veterinarian about your horse's diet when you are changing a ration, are unsure about any feeding practices, or have a horse with special needs. Here are some feeding tips that you may find helpful:

- Feed your horse by weight and work, never by volume.
- Feed at least two times a day, always at the same times.
- Keep water readily available and refill it throughout the day.
- Watch your horse for any changes in mood, coat condition, and manure consistency. These can signal a nutritional deficiency or a digestive problem.
- Store feed and hay in dry, clean, secure locations, such as sealed feed bins and feed rooms, to prevent mold, dust buildup, and insect or rodent infestation.
- Include roughage in your horse's diet. Determine the required amount of forage first and supplement with concentrates.
- Feed horses individually and give each a diet specially formulated to fit his requirements. Any changes must be made over time and not overnight.
- Modify your horse's diet as he ages, loses or gains weight, and changes his level of activity.
- Modify a mare's diet for breeding purposes.
- Don't try to save money by buying poor-quality feed. It can cause health problems and fail to meet your horse's nutritional requirements. This is an area where you need to spend money on your horse. Go by the feed tag, not the price tag.
- Stay on schedule with your pasture management and parasite control programs.

Chapter 3

Horse Sense and Sensibility

Throughout its evolutionary development, from Eohippus to Equus, the horse has perfected the ability to survive. The flight-not-fight instinct is the core of the equine defense system, based on a fast escape from dangerous predators. This instinct eliminates a horse's need to think during an attack and initiates an immediate impulse to run away. Along with this instinct, the horse has exceptional hearing and an enhanced sense of smell that allow him to detect predators from a safe distance. In addition, the horse is one of the fastest of all land mammals. As an owner, you must understand this inborn trait of flight because it affects your horse's ability to learn and the way he behaves and reacts to you and to others.

Equine behavior basics

Your horse doesn't learn from discussions or by imitating behavior; he learns when you reward his good behaviors and punish his bad ones. Horses lack the ability to reason or to make rational, well-thought-out decisions. Their behavior is based on avoiding fear, pain, and domination. As herd animals, horses develop hierarchies and rankings that foster order in their societies. Basically, a hierarchy defines who is in charge and who is not. So, when your horse looks at you, he doesn't see a person. In effect, he sees another horse. He determines whether this new "horse" is his leader or follower, based on the "horse's" behavior toward him. Most well-trained horses look on their owners and trainers as leaders. In dealing with an inexperienced horse that has little or no training, you must immediately establish yourself as his herd leader. You do this by creating a relationship in which you ask him to do something and he does it. Unless you can accomplish this, he will see you as an equal or as below him in rank; in the long run, that could result in a hostile relationship. If your horse is constantly unresponsive to your cues or if he behaves aggressively toward you, consult an experienced trainer who can help you with presenting cues, behavior modification, and humane methods of punishment.

Social behaviors

Horses, like humans, experience a wide range of emotions. Through sounds and body language, they are able to express themselves very effectively. A herd is a horse's family, and all families have ups and downs. Fights usually occur when one horse tries to establish dominance over another horse. The aggressive horse uses his legs to kick and strike, or he bares his teeth to threaten a nasty bite. A stallion fights other stallions over breeding rights and mares; this fight can often be to the death. You should keep stallions out of a mixed herd for the safety of young foals and geldings and never allow stallions free contact with each other. Otherwise, the result could be trouble and injury.

Socialization is very important to a horse's psychological development. When turned out to his pasture, your horse appreciates the presence of at least one other horse. The more horses there are, the more relaxed the herd is; horses live by the saying, "There is safety in numbers." In the wild, mares care for and protect each other's foals from predators. Horses are extremely social animals, forming strong emotional attachments to one another. Like any happy group of friends,

Horses communicate with one another principally through body language. The horse on the left is pinning his ears back to express anger or to show dominance over the other horses.

horses run and play with each other, spend hours eating together, groom and lick one another, even sleep next to each other. If you observe a large group of horses over a period of time, you'll notice certain horses are always together and have formed their own subgroup within the herd. If you remove your horse from his group, he will whinny to let other horses know where he is and to tell them that he is calling for them. One of the worst things you can do to a horse is to isolate him. The only exception is a medical condition. Along with their flight-not-fight instinct, horses have an inherent need to be with other horses. They form their inner spirits and personalities through their daily interaction with other horses. Make sure your horse gets plenty of time with other horses that accept and respect him.

Equine senses

Vision

Even though the horse has extremely large eyes, he actually has very limited sight capabilities. His eyes, placed high on either side of his head, give him a broad field of vision that ranges between 300 and 340 degrees horizontally around his body, but he has two blind spots. One blind spot is two to four feet in front of him, preventing him from seeing his feed, front feet, knees, or anything directly approaching him. The other blind spot is directly behind his hindquarters. When he doesn't know what's going on back there, he can become nervous enough to kick. Your horse's ability to focus depends on the position of his head. To see sharper images, he raises or lowers his head, controlling the amount of light entering his retina and enabling him to focus on objects at different distances. Your horse normally raises his head to focus on things farther away and lowers it to see objects up close.

Species classified as predators have eyes located directly on the front of their head; they use binocular vision to spot potential prey. Humans, big cats, and wolves, for example, use binocular vision to focus on one object while relaying its image to the brain. Species classified as prey animals, including horses, have eyes on the sides of their head; this gives them an enhanced field of vision to detect predators, and the ability to use binocular and monocular vision. Monocular vision allows each of the horse's eyes to see independently of the another. One eye can look to the side while the other looks toward the rear; both images are sent to his brain at the same time, a great advantage when on the lookout for predators. The disadvantage of monocular vision is its lack of depth perception, which causes objects to look flat and distorts their actual distance and height. Although your horse cannot use binocular and monocular vision at the same time, he can instinctively switch from one to the other. For the most part, however, monocular vision dominates. The horse only switches to binocular vision when he needs to focus on one particular object. Researchers believe the actual shift from monocular to binocular vision can make an object appear to jump around in the horse's line of vision, causing him to become startled or spooked. Limited color vision contributes to the horse's inability to recognize common objects. Although your horse can see fairly well in the dark, his eyes need time to adapt to any sudden changes in light. That's why many horses suddenly stop as they are walking in and out of a barn. Their eyes are trying to process the variation in light, which sends them into a protective stance. Once they can focus and adjust to the differences in light, they usually continue walking. Sight plays an important role in your horse's life, affecting his ability to protect himself, his emotional well-being, and his behavior and reactions toward everything around him.

Although stallions commonly display the Flehmen response when they detect the scent of a mare in heat, many horses show it when they smell a new or interesting odor.

Sense of smell

The phrase "a nose always knows" surely applies to a horse. Your horse's sense of smell is his primary means of identification. Without it, he couldn't detect the scent of predators, recognize familiar horses and pastures, select safe water sources and plants, and smell potent reproductive pheromones. When you introduce a new horse into a herd, the other horses inspect and smell him and his manure to make sure he's not a threat and to memorize his scent.

Stallions have one of the most highly developed olfactory systems of any mammal. This acute system increases a stallion's chances of breeding with as many mares as possible. The vomeronasal organ, or Jacobson's organ, contains olfactory receptors that allow a stallion to identify airborne pheromones released from a mare's urine and vaginal secretions, signaling her readiness for breeding. This organ is located in the nasal cavity inside a stallion's mouth. Once he detects the pheromones, the stallion inhales them, causing him to raise his head and curl his lip. This response, called the Flehmen response, sends the enclosed pheromones deeper into his vomeronasal organ where sensory neurons confirm the scent of a fertile and open mare.

Touch

All horses love to be touched. They often go to great lengths to seek out other horses to engage in mutual grooming. Some horses take pleasure in spending hours being rubbed and brushed, enjoying the relaxed feeling that comes from being scratched and massaged. This elevated sense of touch is extremely valuable in protecting and training your horse. Your horse is so sensitive to light touches that he can feel and shake off a single fly using the panniculus muscle beneath his skin or a swift swish of his tail to remove it from his body. Feeling the mild shock of an electric fence lets him know his boundaries and keeps him from challenging the fence. The long whiskers around his muzzle and chin groove help him in identifying close objects and alert him to possible dangers close to his face. In riding or training, use touch to communicate cues and signals. Applying or removing pressure or pain to certain areas of the horse's body instructs him to perform or halt a specific action. After repetitive training, your horse begins to learn how to distinguish between desirable and undesirable pressures and touches. You should always take into account your horse's elevated sense of touch when you exert strong pressure. Too much pressure could cause him to become fearful or angry toward you. Over a long period of time, this leads to a permanent tolerance. The result is unresponsiveness to training and what some trainers call "training numbness."

Hearing

Old Western movies often included a scene where muffled noises are heard and a group of startled horses suddenly lift their heads. They all look in the direction of the noise and begin rearing and running away. In the very next scene, we see a band of howling attackers advancing on horseback. This reaction is based more on truth than fiction. As part of their flight instinct, horses utilize their excellent hearing to protect themselves. Their sharp hearing includes a broad range from the high to the low frequencies. For example, they can hear dangerous predators stalking them from a distance and the vibrating sounds of a distant thunderstorm. Recent studies have determined that a horse hears sounds of up to 25,000 cycles per second. In comparison, a human can only hear sounds of up to 20,000 cycles per second. Your horse's ears increase his chances of survival. His unique ability to rotate each ear independently, about 180 degrees, gives him a wide and accurate hearing range. Since your horse spends the majority of his time grazing with his eyes and nose to the ground, he relies on his hearing to alert him to a possible threat. After lifting his head for further inspection, he quickly assesses the situation and decides whether to stay or run. Your horse's ears are so expressive that the position they are in lets you know what he is feeling. "Pricked" ears, stiff and forward, mean that your horse is on high alert or hears something that has piqued his interest. Ears pinned back are your horse's way of expressing anger or aggression. Always watch your horse's ears when working around him; they help you gauge his mood. Although the length of the ear varies according to the breed, the shape is always the same.

When you are riding or training your horse, he must hear and respond to verbal cues, such as "Whoa" and "No." When giving your commands, speak in a clear and consistent tone and do not yell. Your horse reacts to the intensity and tone of your voice. Many trainers suggest using a gruff, deep tone only when reprimanding or firmly correcting your horse and using a more gentle, pleasant tone when first walking up to him or giving him a verbal cue. Most horses are trained to respond to basic verbal commands, such as "Whoa," "Trot," "Walk," "Canter," "Lope," and "No."

"Pricked" ears, both ears facing forward, usually mean the horse is focusing on a specific sound or trying to hear something directly in front of him.

Bad manners

Biting

Horses bite for several reasons. Young horses bite and nip one another while playing or

Biting does not mean a horse is angry or mean. Many horses give affectionate nips during playtime. You should always watch your horse's ears. If they're pinned back while he's biting, he's not giving you a love nip.

grooming. Stallions fight viciously and bite one another to protect their mares or to show dominance and virility. All horse owners should be concerned about outright aggressive bites toward people and other horses.

Some horses bite after being regularly hand-fed treats and then allowed to use their mouths to search for goodies even when not offered. When a horse doesn't find a treat, he may respond by nipping because he is frustrated. This is absolutely unacceptable and must be corrected. If you're feeding treats to your horse by hand, stop doing so immediately; only offer treats in buckets or pans. If your horse searches for his treat and bites or nips you, make sure you firmly say, "No," and slap his muzzle. Do not hit him with a closed hand and avoid hitting his head. This could eventually lead to a head-shyness problem. As time goes by your horse learns that being mouthy and nipping only leads to an unwelcome slap. If you don't stop minor biting, the habit can progress to vicious biting. An aggressive horse uses biting to dominate and scare you. Many horses start out pinning their ears back and baring their teeth, while others pin their ears and bite at you. Regardless of the type of offensive biting, you must respond immediately by using firm punishment and assertive body language. Since most trainers view biting as the most unacceptable trespass, they suggest that after the initial slap to the muzzle and a loud "No," that you go one step further by reacting like another horse: grunting, squealing, and kicking at his shoulder or flank area. In the worst case scenario, you may need to punish the horse by using a war bridle or stud chain and jerking hard on it when he attempts to bite. The tight pulling and yanking across the horse's gums, nose, and mouth can cause just enough pain to get the point across. Using this method teaches your horse that biting only leads to extreme discomfort. Your horse may need some time to break this nasty habit, but if you think you are not making any progress, consult a professional trainer. For everyone's safety, you should always muzzle a horse with a severe biting problem.

Kicking

A good solid kick from a horse can cause severe injury or even death. Horses kick each other when playing or to express anger or dominance. In a fight, a horse turns his hindquarters to another horse, backs up, and kicks out with both legs in an attempt to do the most damage. You must make sure that your horse knows that even when he is frustrated or angry, you do not tolerate kicking. If your horse kicks or turns his hindquarters preparing to kick you, be ready to respond with a swift punishment. To control the situation, use an open-handed hard smack or the slap of a crop on the hindquarters followed by a loud, "No!" If your horse continues kicking or lifting his leg readying to kick even after punishing him, consider using shackles or kicking chains. Before using chains, ask the advice of a professional trainer. Chains should be a last resort. Place the chains only on the hind legs and buckle them into place around the fetlocks. Every time your horse kicks with his hind legs, the chains hit him, causing a great deal of discomfort. If a horse is a danger to you and others, you must handle him carefully and temporarily separate him from other horses and people.

A horse may also kick as a means of getting attention and releasing built-up energy. Stall-kept horses are prone to kicking out of habit. Animal behaviorists believe stabled horses, who constantly and noisily kick their stall, do it for attention, especially around feeding time. If your horse doesn't like his neighbor, he may kick at him aggressively, regardless of the wall. Most stabled horses are on grain-based diets to increase their energy levels for daily riding or competitions. If they are not regularly turned out or ridden, they find physical release by kicking the stall walls repeatedly. This dangerous form of "exercise" can lead to serious injuries to your horse's legs and hooves. Handle each situation differently, depending on the stimulus for the kicking. If you're not sure of the source of your horse's stall kicking, take the following steps:

◆ Go over to his stall and immediately yell, "NO!" each time you hear your horse kick the walls.

◆ Squirt your horse on his shoulders or legs with a water gun every times he kicks to help deter the habit.

◆ Consider moving any stall neighbors he doesn't get along with. Move in the ones he likes. If he continues to kick at his neighbors, keep him isolated until the kicking stops or lessens. If your horse is a boarder, speak to the stable manager about moving him to another stall as a possible solution.

◆ Cut back on his grain and increase his forage until you can commit to daily exercise or pasture time.

◆ Consider lining the stall walls with padding until your horse curtails his kicking episodes. This reduces the noise level some horses actually seek, helps prevent any injuries, and keeps the walls from being damaged.

◆ Speak to a professional trainer or veterinarian about other ways to treat this unacceptable behavior if all else fails.

Stable vices

Stabled horses indulge in distinctive unsuitable behaviors. Confining a horse to a stall all day limits the amount of exercise, visual stimulation, and socialization he gets. This often leads to frustration and boredom, which translate to repetitive irrational behaviors, hence the term, "stable vices." Horses living out on pasture rarely exhibit these tendencies because they get sufficient exercise, socialization, stimulation from smells and sights, and a diet higher in fiber on a daily basis.

Before buying a new horse, be sure to ask if the horse has any stable vices. You may want to include in your contract or bill of sale that any evidence of a stable vice within thirty days of purchase invalidates the sale and all monies must be returned.

Cribbing

The sound of a horse cribbing is as unique as it is annoying. First, the horse places his upper incisors on a hard object such as a stall door or bucket. Then, he flexes his neck and grunts deeply as he works to fill his pharynx with air. Although the behavior seems to appear when you constantly confine a horse, there are many theories as to what actually triggers cribbing. Some recent studies suggest that a high-grain diet increases the chances of acidosis, which in turn may contribute to a horse's cribbing for physical relief. A horse produces excessive saliva when he cribs. When ingested, the saliva may improve his digestion and decrease hind gut acidity levels.

Researchers also speculate that age and genetics may play important roles in determining whether a horse develops into a cribber. Horses usually begin cribbing at a young age, rarely starting as adults. One possible reason for this could be late weaning practices that leave a young horse with a constant need for the comfort of oral stimulation. Genetics might be another piece of the cribbing puzzle. Although there is not a "cribbing" gene that is passed on, certain personality traits make one bloodline more predisposed to the condition than another. Even though experts are studying and debating different cribbing theories, most veterinarians and behaviorists now agree that cribbing does not cause colic. At one time, they considered cribbing a leading factor in colic cases.

The good news is that cribbing is not some disease spreading like wildfire throughout stables and breeding barns. Very few horses, an estimated 5 to 7 percent, are confirmed cribbers. Although they have no concrete evidence to support their idea, most researchers believe that horses don't learn how to crib from other horses. Still, many owners are nervous about keeping their horse directly across from a cribber.

The only way to ensure your horse never becomes a cribber is prevention. Take steps to reduce the environmental influences that may contribute to cribbing, especially at a young age. Limit and properly balance all grains, increase pasture and exercise time, and keep your horse busy and occupied. The sad reality is that once your horse starts cribbing, stopping it is almost impossible. From then on, you can control the frequency, but you cannot cure it. To treat cribbing, remember the three Ds: direct contact, diet, and distraction. Direct contact may include using a cribbing strap to make your horse very uncomfortable when he tries to flex his neck while taking in air. The strap also makes it difficult for him to do this. Limit your horse's contact with hard objects and textures. Having fewer opportunities available for cribbing assists in controlling and decreasing its occurrence. Other direct treatments that are more costly include electrical shock collars, surgical removal or deadening of specific nerves and muscles in the neck, and drug therapy.

A cribbing horse should spend as much time as possible out on pasture to increase his forage intake and keep him well occupied with grazing. Only feed your horse grain diets if he truly requires the energy for extensive training and competitions. Otherwise, cut back drastically on concentrates and distribute them over several feedings throughout the day. This helps control energy levels and hind gut acidity. You can add herbal supplements, flower essences, and aromatherapy remedies blended for calming and relaxation to his diet or daily care to help reduce the frustration and excitability that encourages cribbing.

Owners sometimes use a cribbing strap to deter a horse from cribbing. The strap, placed tightly behind the poll, restricts the horse's ability to flex his neck, which he has to do in order to gnaw on something.

If a horse isn't thinking about cribbing, he most likely won't do it. Keep a cribbing horse occupied with fun tasks and distractions rather than the wooden stall door or feed bucket. Toys, grazing, riding, and time with other horses are all great ways to take your horse's attention away from the uncontrollable urge to crib, if only for a little while.

Weaving and stall walking

The first reaction most people have when they see a horse weaving is "Why is he dancing?" What looks like a two-step dance in place is really the horse shifting his weight from side to side using his head, neck, and forelegs in a rhythmic and repetitive motion. Boredom, high energy levels, lack of turnout time, and a diet high in grain are all valid reasons why a horse may start to weave.

Stall walking is a vice related to weaving. Some horses repeatedly walk or circle around their stall to release tension and nervousness as a result of being inside all day. They can spend hours pacing back and forth as if in a trance. Stallions typically stall walk, trying to work off sexual frustration and excessive energy. Sometimes by just reworking the energy levels in the feed and giving the horse more exercise time, you can greatly reduce stall walking.

Once a horse starts weaving or stall walking, it can be almost impossible to break the habit. Unlike cribbing, your horse can learn how to weave from watching other horses. Make sure that you keep weavers out of sight of unaffected horses in your barn. No solid evidence exists that stall walking is a learned trait, but you still should keep stall walkers out of view of other horses. Like cribbing, you can reduce the number of weaving and stall-walking episodes, but rarely can you eliminate the habits. To treat weaving and stall walking, behaviorists suggest increasing turnout time with other horses, modifying grain diets by increasing forage intake, using the antidepressant drug clomipramine HCl, and applying other stress-reducing methods available through traditional and holistic therapies. One way to deal with these vices is to get a stall companion, such as a cat or goat. Many famous racehorses have had their own "pets" that traveled with them to various training facilities and racetracks. Stable toys are sometimes able to alleviate boredom and act as a healthy diversion.

Pawing

Pawing, or digging, is more of an annoyance than a serious behavioral problem. Pasture horses often paw the ground when detecting an intriguing scent or before indulging in a good scratch-and-stretch roll. Stabled horses often paw the stall floor for attention or out of boredom and frustration. Many horses paw in anticipation of feeding or as a display of excitement before being turned out. As with other stable vices, pawing can be the result of little exercise time, monotony, a high-energy diet, and the inability to socialize with other horses. Although not considered a significant vice, pawing can ruin stall flooring and wear down your horse's hooves.

If your horse is constantly pawing, put him in a stall with solid flooring, such as wood or concrete. If only clay flooring is available, cover the entire floor with rubber mats. Fill in and cover any open holes formed in the clay floor. Make sure to reprimand your horse when he starts pawing; only reward him when he stops for a lengthy period of time or completely abstains from doing it. If your horse paws when you're about to feed him, don't feed him. Hold the feed to the side and wait till he stops. Bring it to him when he's not pawing. For difficult cases, some traditional trainers may suggest using a stud chain. As your horse begins to paw, jerk down on it just enough to punish him and repeat it if necessary. Since pawing wears on the hooves, discuss different shoeing and hoof care with your farrier. Start with increased outdoor time, stable toys and safety mirrors in his stall, diet adjustments, and a change in the stall flooring. If he continues to paw, try behavioral modification methods, such as verbal reprimands and a series of rewards and punishments. With consistency, understanding, and determination, your horse can stop pawing for good.

Wood chewing

Wood chewing is an extremely bad habit that can be dangerous and destructive. Horses often chew wood fences or doors out of boredom or if their diet is low in fiber and salt. Many owners mistake chewing for cribbing. Cribbing allows a horse to fill his throat with air and flex his muscles, whereas chewing involves actually swallowing and digesting wood particles. This can be life threatening since your horse can easily choke on wood slivers, cut his throat and stomach linings, damage his teeth and gums, and develop a case of impaction colic. If you don't take steps to stop a chewing problem, your horse may eventually progress to cribbing.

The physical damage caused by wood chewing can be very expensive, requiring the replacement of damaged boards, fences, and doors. Help is available to deter your horse from chewing. You can apply special chemicals and sprays directly to the wood, giving it an offensive taste. Some owners put electric wires right above the top line of their wood fences to humanely shock horses trying to get to it. Putting metallic and plastic strips over the tops of fences and doors makes it impossible for your horse to chew down through to the wood. As a last resort, you may need to remove wood fences and install electric or vinyl fencing instead.

Since chewing is a result of boredom, an incomplete diet, or both, you should treat them as equal causes. You can ease boredom with more pasture and socialization time, additional riding or training time, and new stable toys. Give your horse the time he needs to interact with other horses, satisfy his curiosity, and burn off some calories. Increasing roughage and salt intake in your horse's diet may stop his chewing completely. Daily access to grass and hay is extremely important in meeting your horse's demand for fiber, and you can supplement his salt intake with a salt block or by adding it to his feed. If diet is the main cause of his chewing, supplementing it should eliminate the habit for good. Many of the various nutritional supplements on the market can help reduce or stop chronic chewing. Once you have exhausted all of these remedies without success, consult your veterinarian for other possible methods of dealing with this problem. If left untreated, wood chewing can result in a serious medical condition.

Bolting feed

Bolting means the horse rapidly swallows his grain without chewing it, causing him to choke or become colicky. Large amounts of whole feed can get stuck in your horse's throat or lodged deep within his digestive tract, forming an impaction colic. A horse may start bolting his grain because of extreme hunger, an unbalanced diet, irregular feeding times, or constant nervousness.

If you believe your horse is bolting his feed, take immediate steps to stop it. Special feeders are available that can help slow down his eating by only allowing him access to small amounts of feed at a time. Putting large rocks or salt blocks into the feeder can help slow down his eating because he must move them around to get to his feed. As a first course, feed hay in a hay net with small openings to keep your horse busy as well as to help satisfy his initial hunger before you give him his grain. Most importantly, feed your horse consistently and on a strict schedule. Regular feedings reduce his craving for food, help his digestion, and calm any anxieties or frustrations that arise from being very hungry. Once you take these steps, you have reduced the chance of your horse choking or becoming colicky, but the bolting problem may still persist.

If he is bolting because he's not getting enough feed speak to your veterinarian about adjusting and increasing your horse's diet. Be honest with your veterinarian; he needs to know exactly what your horse has and hasn't been eating. Given the right information, your veterinarian can create a balanced diet based on your horse's age, sex, and level of activity. If he is bolting, many veterinarians suggest feeding your horse chaff, a special blend of finely cut or chopped hay to add bulk and filler to his feeding. The chaff's texture forces your horse to chew and swallow, which satisfies his appetite and also reduces the nervousness many bolters get when they are hungry. Depending on the type of chaff you use, your veterinarian may suggest mixing it with grain or using it to replace a portion of your horse's grain ration. Until the bolting slows down or stops, you must feed your horse under special conditions, carefully supervising him when he is eating.

Stable toys

Stable toys seem to be the new craze for stall-kept horses. Since veterinarians and equine behaviorists cite boredom as the primary cause of stable vices, toys can offer hours of distraction and amusement. Horses can kick balls around in a stall or paddock, and they can push or knock around toys hung from the wall or ceiling. Rolling toys reward the horse with pellets, and a safety mirror gives him something to look at.

These items are available at horse supply stores and through mail-order catalogs. Stable toys are definitely not substitutes for letting your horse run around a pasture to play with stablemates, but they do make his time in the stall a bit more interesting.

Safety around horses

Here are a few basic safety tips to keep in mind when working around your horse:

- Be aware of where you position yourself around your horse.
- Stay close to your horse and keep a hand on him at all times, letting him know where you are.
- Do not yell or shout at your horse. Raise your voice only to reprimand.
- Always approach your horse from the side so he can see you, never from directly in front of him or behind him.
- Stay calm and self-assured at all times. Horses can sense fear and nervousness in handlers.

Body positioning and hand placement

Horses are fast movers when they are angry or scared. They can have their hindquarters facing you dead on in seconds. For your protection, know the safety areas around any horse, the correct way to move and walk about a horse, and how to use your hands as a means of communication and as safety tools.

As mentioned before, always stay close to your horse and keep a hand on him at all times. This isn't for affection. The closer you are to him, the harder it is for him to get in a full kick, which causes the most serious injuries. Hands on his shoulders and hindquarters help push you away as your horse moves to kick. Forming a loose fist helps push you even farther away when your horse turns quickly or kicks. Keeping a hand on your horse lets him know you are there, even if he can't see you very well. It tells him, "I am here, don't be scared, and no kicking, please."

The safest place around a horse is next to his shoulders. When approaching a horse, always walk toward his left shoulder. Keep in mind, however, that the shoulder area is not a guaranteed safe spot; you must remain alert. Horses rarely kick out with their forelegs. They normally use these for striking while rearing in fear or anger. If your horse rears up, quickly move to safety, at least fifteen to twenty feet away.

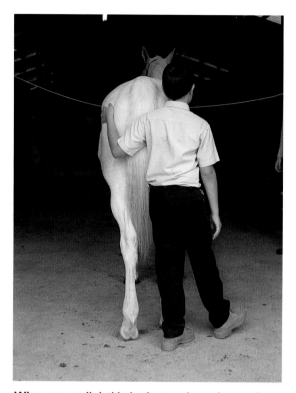

When you walk behind a horse, always keep a hand on him and keep your body as close to him as possible.

Never stand directly behind your horse; this is a blind spot, and it is inside his kicking range. If you need to work on his tail or groom down the back end, try to stand to the side and face the rear. One hand can hold his tail, and the other hand can brush while you stand next to his hindquarters.

If you need to move to the other side of your horse, you have two ways to do this safely. The most common practice is to keep a hand and a bent elbow on your horse and to walk quickly and calmly right behind his hindquarters. Have your body as close to your horse as possible. Your hand lets him know you're there, the bent elbow and close body position keep you out of his kicking range, and the steady pace limits his reaction time.

If this method makes you uneasy, walk completely outside his kicking range, approximately twenty feet behind him. Inexperienced and impatient owners often disregard safety when they decide to move to the opposite side of their horse by crawling underneath the barrel or ducking under his neck area. Both of these approaches are dangerous. Crawling beneath his barrel frightens the horse because he can't see underneath himself, especially when tied up. When you move this way, he could accidentally kick and trample you. Because your horse has a blind spot directly in front of him, he can't see you duck under his neck. This can cause him to spook and rear within perfect striking range. Many owners have been seriously injured because they carelessly moved from one side of the horse to the other. Do not risk your life for the few seconds it takes to walk behind your horse properly.

Sacking out

The term "sacking out" refers to the process of desensitizing horses to common objects and sounds that frighten them. The practice began over a century ago when horsemen rubbed and shook empty flour and potato sacks on and around their horses. Their aim was to help their horses accept the sack with a calm and quiet stance. In today's training programs, sacking out is still one of a yearling's first training lessons. It teaches a young horse how to behave around new objects and sounds without panicking. A horse that spooks at every noise and strange object, and is permitted to get away with it, can become a risky and unpleasant mount.

Trainers suggest beginning a sacking-out session by rubbing objects all over your horse, such as bright towels and blankets. The feel and sight of colorful fabrics are an ideal way to start getting your horse used to various stimuli. Allow your horse to move around on a lead rope or lunge line within a circle as you rub and shake the materials around him. For the first part of the session, all he wants to do is move around or run away. Do not allow him to pull or move out of the designated circle. Be adamant about moving him in a tight circle as you continue to introduce the blankets or towels. After a while, he should begin to relax and realize he is not in danger from these objects. Finally, he should be able to accept them. At that point, he should have no problem having these items placed on his back, rubbed on his face, and waved up and down. When you next come back to a sacking-out session, he should

Plastic shopping bags are useful for "sacking out" your horse. The crinkling sounds they make provoke interesting reactions and responses during a training session.

still be completely at ease around those objects. If not, start again and continue until he is at ease with them.

As he becomes more receptive to objects on and around him, gradually progress to new sounds and strange surroundings. Plastic shopping bags are great for first-time sack outs that focus on sound. Not only do they feel funny when rubbed on your horse, they also make a soft but distinct sound when crumpled or shaken. Once your horse has completely accepted one sound, you can introduce a new one. Try not to introduce more than one noise at a time. The key to successful sacking out is consistency and understanding on your part. No matter how scared your horse acts, keep putting that scary object on him and in front of him. Sacking out is a perfect way for you to teach your horse the lessons of acceptance and adaptation. When presenting new things, try to relate to your horse's fears by remembering that he can't reason for himself what the objects are. Don't get frustrated if he is nervous and wants to move around. Keep with him, be patient, and he will eventually get it.

Imprinting

Imprinting is the first training lesson for a young foal. Many horse trainers believe that human contact is necessary within the first two hours of a foal's birth in order to gain his acceptance. The true objective of imprinting is to accustom your foal to your touch, smell, and voice in order to gain his trust and later on to establish yourself as a leading herd member. Although many owners have claimed great success with imprinting, others have found that it doesn't make any difference. Animal behaviorists have completed several studies on imprinting foals, but they have not been able to prove or disprove the effectiveness of imprinting. In general, most veterinarians favor imprinting a healthy foal, stressing that it doesn't hurt to do so. Once the mare has had time to clean off her foal and bond with him, a positive imprinting session can help a foal adapt to being around humans. It also teaches your mare to accept you and others working around her and her foal on a regular basis. Be aware that an aggressively protective mare could react violently or irrationally if she fears for her foal's safety and is not used to the constant presence of people.

Good manners

Your well-mannered horse should be able to stand calmly in stocks or cross-ties or tied to a solid fence post without fidgeting or pawing, espe-

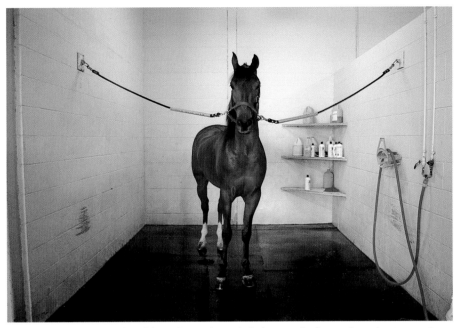

Cross-ties clipped to the sides of your horse's halter make it much easier to work on your horse when you are bathing, clipping, and grooming him and during farrier visits. To prevent severe injuries, you should never leave your horse unattended while he is in cross-ties.

cially when the farrier or veterinarian has to work on him or treat him. The stock is a walk-in structure used for restraining purposes. Its pipe or metal sides limit your horse's side-to-side movement. The front and back of the stock are closed off with rope, safely boxing your horse in. For everyone's safety, veterinary procedures such as drawing blood and vaccinations are usually accomplished in the stock. Cross-ties and tying your horse using a quick-release knot are more suitable for general grooming and bathing. If your horse isn't used to these measures of control and to standing in one place for a long time, start getting him used to it. Groom or bathe your horse using all three methods, and soon they will become part of his normal routine. Be sure to praise him when he behaves well under restraint and reprimand him if he starts pawing or shaking his head out of annoyance.

Lifting feet

Your horse should be willing to have his front and back feet picked up when asked or when you pull them up. At any age, your horse can learn to lift his feet when cued. Because his hooves are vital components of his conformation and are common sites for injuries and infections, a farrier and veterinarian must be able to examine them easily. Since these professionals usually don't have the time or patience to persuade your horse to lift his feet, it's up to you to teach him to cooperate and to show good manners.

Front feet

◆ Begin by standing next to your horse's shoulder as you face his hindquarters. Place your inside hand (the hand closest to the horse) on his shoulder for safety purposes.

◆ Bend over slightly and repeatedly run your outside hand gently downward from his lower leg to his hoof. Speak to him in a gentle tone, reassuring him you're not a threat.

◆ After about five downward strokes, use your outside hand to grip your horse's pastern as you lean into his shoulder. This makes him shift his weight to the other foreleg and makes it much easier for you to lift his foot.

◆ Reinforce your cue by saying, "Lift" or "Give" as you raise his foot.

◆ Do not elevate his foot too high because this can cause discomfort or a loss of balance. Lift it up just enough that you can comfortably bend or kneel slightly as you carefully lean against his shoulder.

◆ While holding his foot up, switch his pastern from your outside hand to your inside hand. Firmly cup or hold the foot with your inside hand. You can hold his entire foot to the side of your legs or move it between your legs, gently squeezing it into place right above your knees. Farriers typically place the front hoof between their legs, allowing them the use of both hands while working, or they use a

Hold the hoof up at a comfortable level and cup it gently in your hand. Try not to pull the leg and hoof too far back. Doing so may cause your horse to lose his balance or become nervous.

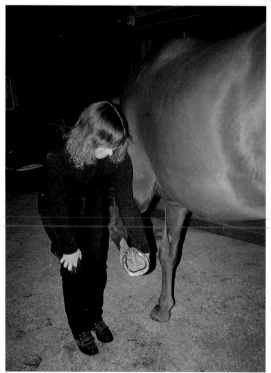

foot stand so that the hoof faces forward and rests on it. When cleaning hooves, most owners just hold the foot next to their legs while leaning into their horse and using a hoof pick.

◆ Keep the foot lifted for one to two minutes; slowly lower it down. Praise your horse. After a short rest, repeat the steps a few more times and quit for the day.

◆ For training purposes, practice both holding methods until your horse is comfortable with each. After several training sessions, your horse will automatically start picking up his front feet when feeling downward strokes or pressure on his pastern and when given a verbal cue.

Hind feet

◆ Because the hindquarters are the most powerful part of your horse, you must be cautious and alert when working with his hind feet.

◆ Start by facing the rear while standing close to your horse's hind leg or flank. Place the hand closest to his body onto his hip and begin bending over slightly as you move your other hand down the back of his leg to his fetlock.

◆ Loosely grasp his fetlock, pull his foot forward, and gently lift up his hind leg for better positioning.

◆ Reinforce your cue by saying, "Lift" or "Give" as you raise his foot.

◆ At this point, you can either move your inside leg under his hind leg, placing his hind foot between your legs and above your knees, or you can allow the lower part of his hind leg to rest upon your bent thighs.

◆ Once his leg is in place,

When lifting your horse's hind foot, be sure you position your body correctly on the side of the hind leg and not in front of it. Gently raise his leg as you lean against him and reinforce the cue by saying, "Lift." Place his lower leg on top of your thigh.

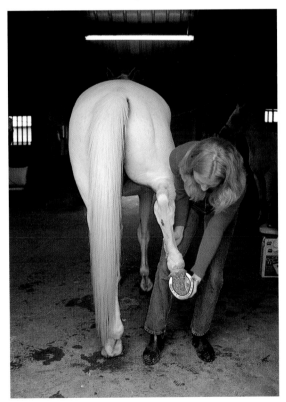

bend your knees into a comfortable position and steady his hoof with one hand while you pick his hoof clean with your other hand.

◆ Gently move his leg off your thigh or around your inside leg and set his foot down. Praise your horse for his cooperation.

◆ Practice both stances with your horse so he is calmly prepared for each one. Eventually, as with the forelegs, your horse automatically begins to lift his hind legs after feeling your strokes or a gentle lift.

Catching a loose horse

There is a right way and a wrong way to catch a horse in his pasture or paddock. If you use the wrong way, you may spend hours running around, or your horse may spook or bolt, risking injury to both of you. If enough people have handled your horse, he should accept being approached and haltered, but he has his own rules on being caught, and you need to respect them.

Spot your horse and begin walking toward him at a steady pace. Hold the unbuckled halter attached to a lead rope that's neatly gathered on your shoulder or held at your side. Do not walk straight into his front blind spot. Instead, walk up at an angle toward his left shoulder.

To catch your horse, walk at a steady, calm pace toward him. Never run or yell when approaching him. Extend your hand toward his muzzle so that he is able to smell your distinctive scent.

Put the lead rope around your horse's neck before you put the halter on so that you have more control over his head and neck and can prevent him from trying to walk off. Don't put the lead rope too far forward on his neck.

As you get close, say your horse's name calmly, letting him hear you. Put your hand out toward his nose for him to identify your scent. Gently pet his neck as you move a few steps forward just in front of his left shoulder.

Turn your body toward his neck. Use one hand to hold the unbuckled halter and your other hand to place the end of the lead rope over his neck. You can now use the lead rope to control his neck and prevent him from walking off.

Turn your body to face his front. Put your hands on both side straps of the halter or place your left hand on the buckle band and your right hand on the lower portion of the crownband. Position your right arm underneath his neck as you prepare to put on his halter.

Pull the halter upward, allowing its noseband to rest on his upper muzzle.

While holding up the halter, move your left hand up to the buckle. Use your right hand to push over the untwisted crownband to his left side and across the poll area behind his ears.

Move your right hand to grasp the end of the crownband while your left hand holds up the buckle and its latch. Make sure you have not positioned the crownband too far up or down from the poll.

Insert the crownband into the buckle, pulling it gently and inserting

With the halter correctly positioned on your horse's head, buckle the crownband in one of the middle holes. Check that the lead-rope clip is securely attached to the halter and gently remove the lead rope from your horse's neck.

the latch into a loophole that is midway between loose and tight. The halter fit should be tight enough to stay in a good position while giving you control of your horse's head. As a rule, you should easily be able to slide two fingers underneath the noseband.

Don't forget to slip the slack of the crownband through the buckle's lower end and gently pull the lead rope lying over his neck toward you. Praise your horse for his cooperation.

Leading and turning your horse

Start walking once the halter is on and the lead rope is safely off his neck and in your hands. Always be aware of your body position and distance from your horse, keeping your body close to his neck area, behind his poll, and in front of his left shoulder. Staying in this safe outside position keeps you from walking too far forward or backward, which can limit your control and visual field.

Place your right hand on the lead rope just below where the snap attaches to the halter. Hold the neatly gathered slack of the lead rope in your left hand. Never wrap the slack of the rope around your hand because if your horse decides to bolt, he will drag you with him.

Begin to step forward and say, "Walk." Your horse should be walking at your pace, not his. If he moves ahead or seems to be just

While walking your horse and holding the lead rope, pull your right arm underneath his neck, directing him to move his entire body away from you.

Continue to walk at a steady pace and lean into your horse as you turn. Once you've completed the turn, straighten out and proceed at the current pace or stop safely.

dragging his hooves, correct this by turning him in a circle first and adjusting his pace to yours when walking forward.

Do full or half turns from a complete standstill or as you're walking.

Maintain your body and hand positions as if you were going to walk a straight path. You always want to move your horse to the right so that your body remains in an outside position.

Hold the top of the lead rope with your right hand and move your right arm underneath your horse's neck, pulling his head away from you and to the right.

Keep moving toward the right with your horse as he bends his neck to the right, leaning into him slightly. This maintains his movement away from you during the turn.

Return your body to a safe leading position after you have completed the turn.

Backing up your horse

Your horse needs to know how to walk backward just as he needs to know how to walk forward. Ultimately, your horse should be willing to back up when cued on a lead rope, while being ridden, and when stepping off a trailer. Horses aren't scared about moving backward, but it's not something they do very often unless they're about to kick. Again, be aware of your body position when beginning to move your horse backward. Trainers often advise backing your horse up if he tries to walk past you or when you're correcting a training exercise.

- ◆ Check to make sure that the halter fits properly and that the rope snap is secure.
- ◆ Walk your horse in the correct leading position while in your safety zone by his neck. Stop your horse.
- ◆ Stay in the neck-shoulder area as you turn your body around to face his left shoulder. Never stand right in front of your horse. Move your left hand onto the lead rope just below the snap. Hold the rest of the rope in your right hand.
- ◆ Begin pulling or jerking your left hand toward his body and push your weight forward into his shoulder, taking one or two steps. At the same time, use the end of the lead rope as a stimulus, tapping it against his shoulder. Making kissing or clicking sounds may help to reinforce your cues. Always say, "Back up" as you initiate the action.
- ◆ Keep at it and don't give up. Make sure he takes two to four steps back and then praise him.
- ◆ You'll have an easier time backing up your horse if you use a bit and bridle, but a halter along with consistent cues and body language can work just as well. Most horses start to learn fairly quickly that when you turn and face them at the shoulder, you

When asking your horse to back up, stand at his left shoulder, never directly in front of him. Standing in front of him can be extremely dangerous. Lean your body weight forward and use the end of the lead rope to apply gentle taps against his shoulder to encourage him to step backwards.

want them to back up. After enough practice, your horse should do it very easily with very little incentive needed.

Tying your horse

There may be times when you won't have access to cross-ties, stocks, or a paddock when you want to work around your horse. If your horse spooks while tied incorrectly, he could seriously injure his neck and back. Knowing where and how to safely tie your horse prevents any mishaps.

Never tie your horse to fence boards, hollow objects, or door handles. They can't withstand the pull of a thousand-pound horse. Instead, tie your horse to objects that are reinforced, such as fence posts, steel railings, hooks on stall walls or in trailers, or to secured brass wall rings. Although a breakaway halter is primarily a tool for halter training, think about using it if your horse has a habit of constantly rearing or pulling when tied. These halters split open under extreme pressure when a horse rears or pulls back, preventing him from injuring himself.

The quick-release knot is a must when tying your horse to a solid

The quick-release knot.

object. When you pull on the end of the lead rope, the knot opens quickly. There are different ways to tie quick-release knots. Here is one version:

◆ Check to make sure you have securely attached the lead-rope snap to the metal ring in the halter's chin strap.

◆ Choose a solid hitching object and pick a good area around it where you can easily tie the rope. Your horse should be able to stand with his head at a comfortable height, not too high or too low. He should also be able to move his head slightly from side to side and up and down, but he should not be able to walk backward or forward.

◆ Take the end of the lead rope and pull it around the solid object. Leave twelve to fifteen inches of slack between your horse and where the rope begins to wrap around the solid object. Once you have positioned it correctly, take the end of the lead rope and move it underneath and across the portion of rope connected to the halter, "the halter rope." The two sections of rope create a loop around the hitching object.

◆ Make another tight loop with the end of the lead rope. Pull that loop over the halter rope and through the existing loop around the hitching object, until some rope remains outside the loop. This extra portion of rope opens the knot when you pull it.

◆ Pull the loop around the hitching object and the halter rope at the same time to center the knot. Wrap one hand around the top of the halter rope, where it meets the end of the loop around the hitching object. Put your other hand on the lower part of the halter rope. At the same time, push your wrapped hand upward toward the loop and pull your other hand toward you, tightening the knot into place. Test the rope to make sure it stays in place.

◆ To undo the knot, pull the hanging section of rope, and the knot automatically releases. Pull or remove the lead rope from the hitching object.

Releasing your horse

When you are finished riding for the day and are ready to return your horse to his pasture, be sure to buckle a halter loosely around his neck first. Then, tie him to a solid object using the quick-release knot. Remove his bridle and place it over your shoulder. Move his halter forward and place it on his head correctly. Take off the rest of his tack and finish up with a relaxing walk, a wash down, or some grooming time.

Lead your horse into the pasture, but don't rush it. He should be able to stand by you calmly with the halter on, even with his urge to run freely and roll around. When you're ready, unbuckle his halter and slip it off his head. Pat him on the neck as praise. Many horses stand by their owners until the owners turn to walk away. You don't want your horse to get into the bad habit of pulling or trying to run off when he's about to be released.

When bringing your horse back into his stall, walk him in and turn him around to face the door. He should wait patiently for you to remove his halter and not go immediately for the feed bucket or hay net. Make sure he behaves himself, especially when you are in the stall with him. Once you remove the halter, give him a good pat and walk out.

Loading your horse into and out of a trailer

Many owners seem to think that horse trailers are only for show horses and sport horses. True, owners must have trailers to get from one event to another, but all horses should be able to load into and unload out of a trailer. The time will come when you must transport your horse in one, whether you're moving, going to a show, or taking your horse to a veterinary hospital. Horse trailers come in a variety of styles with many features, and are priced accordingly. Many trailers come with tack and storage rooms furnished with heating and air-conditioning units. The most important things to look for in a trailer are excellent ventilation and secure locks and latches. In addition to a well-built trailer, you'll need a reliable vehicle that has the horsepower to pull it. If you can't afford a trailer, you can find many professional horse-transporting companies to trailer your horse for a fee or to rent you a trailer.

Starting at a young age, every horse should learn how to load onto a trailer. When buying a new horse, inquire about how well he loads and unloads and ask for a demonstration. For an experienced show horse, his trailer is like a second home. He should walk on with ease. If you've never loaded a horse before, do not wait until the day of a show or veterinarian appointment to start teaching him. As with any type of horse training, the more you practice, the easier the exercise gets. Ultimately, your horse should be able to walk calmly up to the open trailer and load right onto it with little assistance and without a poor attitude.

How you load your horse depends on the type of trailer you are using. A basic stock trailer, used mostly for livestock, has open slats all around and no dividers. It's not ideal for transporting a horse. The design of most common two-horse trailers allows for straight loading from the back with either a permanent divider or a divider that adjusts to a straight or side position. Trailers that can hold more than two horses usually load into a side position to utilize the entire space, but they limit your access on entering the trailer with your horse. Trailer doors, designed with safety locks and easy-to-use latches, are in the back and open outward. The two methods discussed below are based on loading your horse onto a two-horse trailer with either straight or side-adjusting dividers, no ramp, and only rear access:

Hitch the trailer to your truck as instructed by the manufacturer and check that all trailer lights are working. Set the emergency brakes for both your truck and trailer.

Open the back doors and make sure the trailer floor is clean and lined with a rubber mat, wood shavings, or both. Put some hay into a feeder or set up a hay net. Having hay accessible sometimes helps motivate your horse to enter the trailer and keeps him occupied during the trip. Ask a friend to stand by in case you need some help.

Lead your horse toward the open trailer. Begin walking him at least fifteen feet behind the trailer to get him up to a steady pace.

Method A: If you are able, walk into the trailer with him, holding his lead rope as you step into the trailer. Walk forward on the left side of the divider, leading him onto the right side of the trailer. Tie him securely inside the trailer, especially if you are loading another horse onto the other side.

Method B: If you are unable to enter the trailer with him or if he is an experienced loader, take off his lead rope and walk him to the trailer holding the left cheek strap of his halter. Keep a steady pace. As you reach the entrance, keep your hand on the halter and pull him forward, leading his head inside and coaxing him to keep moving forward into the trailer. Release your hand from the halter, step slightly to the side,

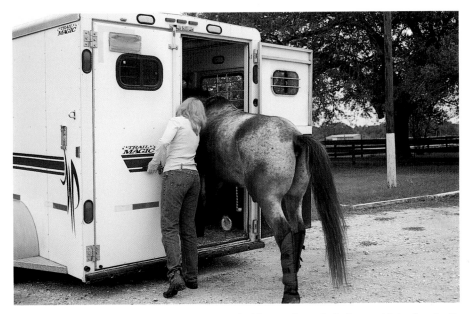

This method of loading requires that you hold your horse's halter until he has both front feet in the trailer. As he moves farther inside, release your hand and secure him in place.

and turn your body away as he steps into the trailer. Move the adjustable divider to secure him into place.

Close and lock the trailer doors.

Method A is ideal for a horse first learning how to get into the trailer, for one who has issues about trailers, or for an owner with limited trailer-loading experience. If you're able and willing to walk onto the trailer with your horse, by all means do so. Eventually, you'll want to advance him from Method A to Method B. If you learn one thing from all this, it's not to rush the loading process. If you get too frustrated or angry, your horse will know it and start shying away from trailer loading altogether. Be very patient and take your time with it. Remember to praise your horse through every step; this reinforces his efforts and reduces his fears when it comes to loading. When he gets to the trailer, say, "Good boy," and when he takes a step into the trailer, say, "Good boy" again. Keep praising him until you lock the trailer doors.

Horses usually acquire loading problems as a result of inconsistent training methods and by learning which actions can help them avoid getting onto the trailer. Trainers say that the problem is not that a horse can't get into a trailer; the problem is that he just doesn't want to, and your job is to tell him that he must. If you don't do your job, he won't do his. Be firm but understanding when it comes to loading. Practice and let your horse take his time becoming used to the process. If he acts up, reprimand him and make it clear that he must behave himself when in or around the trailer. A good idea is to ask some experienced friends to help you load, especially to assist from behind your horse. Often when a horse is loading, he gets his forefeet in and then wants to back out. If this happens, get those forefeet in, and have one or two friends hold a lead rope across his thighs and gaskins. As he steps in, have your friends move to either side of him while holding the rope and forcing his back end into the trailer. Be ready to tie him to the front of the trailer.

Unloading is much easier than loading. Most horses are eager to exit the trailer and get onto steady ground. However, you don't want your horse rushing off the trailer. This is unsafe, and it displays bad manners. Your horse should be able to stand in the trailer calmly while you untie him and open the trailer doors. Follow the same steps as if you were backing him up, making sure he takes slow steps, especially when stepping down. If you can't enter the trailer, open the trailer doors, pat him on the rump, and let him see the exit. If your horse knows the verbal cue, have someone go to the front window or vent and say, "Back up" a

After you open the back door, give your horse time to step out of the trailer. Experienced horses will usually come right out, but horses just learning about unloading will need your patience and some encouragement to back out.

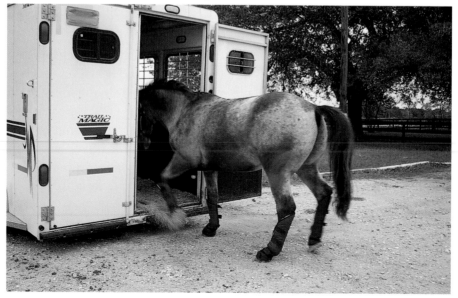

few times. When a horse is new to unloading, you may need several attempts before he learns how to back out, but in due time, he'll figure it out. Once your horse has loaded and unloaded several times, you will both settle into a comfortable routine.

Adjusting to a new stall or a show stall

Changes, such as meeting new horses, smelling unfamiliar scents, and tasting strange water, can cause complete panic in some horses. This can affect the health and performance of horses new to the show circuit. Of course, some horses are never upset by new surroundings, but most horses find it difficult to adjust to a different schedule and strange environment. You can make it easier for your horse to transition to a new stall or show stall. Here are some tips:

- ◆ Use the same type of shavings he's used to, even if this means bringing your own.
- ◆ Bring jugs of water from your barn's water supply.
- ◆ Don't change his diet. Try to bring hay, alfalfa, and grain from your own stock.
- ◆ Spray aromatherapy or flower essence blends to reduce his stress or nervousness.
- ◆ Bring your horse's stable toy with you.
- ◆ Rub his blanket over horses he's friendly with to get their scent on it.
- ◆ Check on him and be sure to give him lots of attention.

Communicating with your horse

Horses speak their own language, one that defines who they are and their way of life. Instead of just speaking at them, you also need to listen and hear them. You need to try and learn their language through watching and listening to the way they interact with each other. Understanding the basics of their behaviors, sensory systems, pecking orders, and learning abilities can help you in your quest to correctly communicate with and train your horses. Always keep in mind that a horse is an incredible creature that took millions of years to perfect. Accept what he is by understanding his shortcomings, his flight instinct, his sight limitations, and his need to find his place in the world through dominance and fear. After accepting these drawbacks, work to suppress his weaknesses and nurture his strengths in order to develop the very best training program.

Progressive trainers have always suggested that you speak *to* your horse and not *at* him. Start thinking and acting like a horse by envisioning his mindset. Look at each training lesson as a friendly game of chess. In order to win, you need to be smart enough to contemplate the next move and to respond accordingly. Get inside your horse's head and learn what his personality is like, what scares him, which horses he socializes with, etc. The more understanding you have of your horse, the easier it is to communicate with him. Of course, you absolutely must establish yourself as his herd leader before becoming his teacher and friend, but with patience, consistent training methods, and commitment, you no longer have to "break" your horse. Instead, you can create a relationship based on respect and mutual understanding.

Chapter 4

Understanding Your Horse's Health

One of the greatest challenges you face as a horse owner is keeping your horse healthy. Unfortunately, many diseases, conditions, and injuries can harm and even kill your horse. For his sake, you must be able to recognize symptoms, take vital signs, and give first aid. Select a nearby equine veterinarian you trust. A good veterinarian treats your horse effectively and educates you on how to improve your horse's health. Without a doubt, a sick horse is an expensive horse. In the long run, investing in yearly vaccinations, health exams, and a first-aid kit benefits both you and your horse.

Your ability to recognize early signs and effectively manage emergency situations could save your horse's life. The first signs your horse isn't feeling well are ones you will observe. Is he eating? What is his behavior? Is he less active and alert? These are just some of the questions to think about when looking over your horse. Remember, you are the best judge of whether your horse is well or not, and your veterinarian depends on your observations to help determine what the problem is.

Vital signs

If you suspect your horse isn't well, the first thing to do is check his vital signs: temperature, pulse, and respiration. Write them down and indicate the time you took them. Many veterinarians ask for this information when you call.

The normal temperature range for horses is between 99 and 101.5 degrees F. You need to take your horse's temperature rectally. Try and take his temperature when he is at complete rest. Taking his temperature after riding could result in a reading almost 3 degrees higher than it really is.

Use a digital thermometer. They are accurate, durable, and very safe. If you use a glass thermometer, you run the risk of it breaking, and the mercury leaking out.

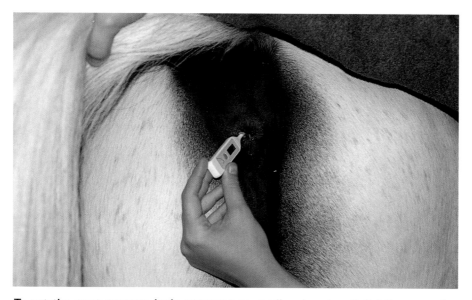

To get the most accurate body temperature reading, insert a digital thermometer about halfway into your horse's rectum. Hold the thermometer in place until you get a reading.

Place the thermometer only about halfway into your horse's rectum, and hold on to it. The muscles around the horse's rectum are very strong and can pull the thermometer all the way in. Most digital thermometers beep when the temperature reading is complete. Remember to wipe the thermometer off with alcohol after every use. If your horse has a temperature of 102 degrees F for twenty-four hours, is lethargic, not eating, or in discomfort, call your veterinarian.

A horse's normal heart rate ranges from 30 to 50 beats per minute, but the average is 28 beats per minute. The easiest way to determine your horse's heart rate is to use a stethoscope. To listen for heartbeats, place the stethoscope behind his elbow, count the beats for thirty seconds, and then multiply by two.

If you don't have a stethoscope, you can use your fingers. Place two fingers on the facial artery, located in the lower jaw area. Once you can feel the pulse, count it for thirty seconds and then multiply by two.

The final vital sign is respiration. Normal respiration for a horse at rest is eight to sixteen breaths per minute. The most obvious way to get a horse's respiration is to watch his rib cage rise and fall. Count a full breath from when your horse inhales to when he exhales. Count the breaths for thirty seconds and then multiply by two. Another way to get an accurate respiration reading is by placing your hand over one of your horse's nostrils and feeling the breaths. Count the breaths for thirty seconds and then multiply by two.

An elevated heart rate is quite common in unfit or less active horses. Athletic horses normally have lower heart and respiration rates because of their conditioning and better fitness. An elevated respiration rate, especially in hot climates, could mean your horse is suffering from heat stress. If your horse is struggling to breathe or is gasping, call your veterinarian immediately.

Other vitals to check

Gut Sounds: Lack of gut sounds could be the first sign of colic. You should hear rumbling or gurgling when you place your ear to your horse's barrel or listen

To determine your horse's heart rate, find the facial artery located underneath his jaw, hold his head still, and begin counting his pulse for at least thirty seconds. The average heart rate is 28 beats per minute.

You can determine the respiration rate for a horse at rest by feeling and counting breaths. Place your hand just below your horse's nostrils while holding his head in position. Do not cover the nostrils completely or you will interfere with his ability to exhale.

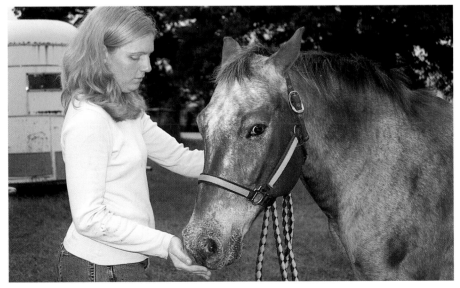

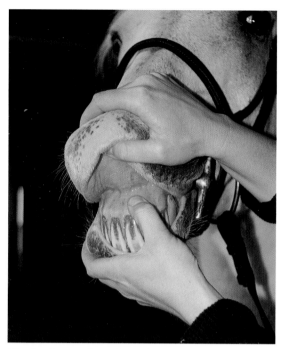

To check your horse's capillary refill, gently lift his upper lip and press on his gum. A slow rate of return of gum color could indicate a circulatory problem or dehydration.

with a stethoscope. If you don't hear any noises, look for his feces in a stall or paddock. If you don't find any fresh manure, call your veterinarian.

Fecal Passage: If your horse hasn't passed any feces within twelve to twenty-four hours, this could be a sign of obstructive colic.

Capillary Refill: To assess your horse's blood circulation, check his gum color; it should be pink. Abnormal gum colors are red, white, and bluish purple. If your horse's gums are bluish purple, call your veterinarian immediately. After checking gum color, lift your horse's lip and press your thumb against the gums. The gums should turn white but then return to a pink color in two or three seconds. If it takes longer than that, your horse could be in distress.

Skin Pliability: To measure the hydration of your horse's skin, pinch the skin on his neck. After you release the skin, it should snap back quickly. If it doesn't return quickly, this could be an indication that your horse is dehydrated. Another reliable sign of dehydration is sunken eyes.

Other Signs: Other immediate signs to look for are a discharge around the eyes and nose, lack of appetite, and unusual behavior.

Infectious diseases

Like most domesticated animals, horses are susceptible to infectious diseases. Living in groups in rural environments increases their exposure to diseases and their carriers. Although not all diseases can be prevented, vaccinations and veterinary care can prevent many of them. This is why you must have your horse vaccinated regularly and have him examined yearly by a veterinarian.

Equine infectious anemia (EIA)

Bloodsucking insects and dirty needles transmit equine infectious anemia (EIA) or "swamp fever," a serious viral infection. You can confirm an EIA infection through a blood test, the Coggins test, which verifies the presence of EIA antibodies. The disease can manifest itself in three forms: carrier, chronic, and acute. An EIA carrier has a positive Coggins result and shows little or no symptoms. A chronic case often has weight loss, anemia, fever, and a lack of appetite. Most chronic carriers experience a period during which symptoms come and go, but eventually the horse becomes an acute case. An acute case of EIA has high fever, jaundice, weakness, and edema, leading to death. No vaccine is available for EIA, but pharmaceutical companies are trying to develop one. At the present time, the number of EIA horses in the United States is low, and steps are being taken to control and limit the spread of the disease.

If you show your horse, you must present a negative Coggins test taken within the last twelve months. Some shows require a Coggins test within the last six months. Check with the show management to be sure. Regardless of the requirements for a specific show, your horse should have a Coggins test every year. Horses that test positive for EIA can have another test thirty days later, but if the retest is also positive, the horse is certified as infected with EIA. You must quarantine an EIA positive horse a minimum of two hundred yards from other horses, mules, and donkeys for the remainder of the horse's life. An infected horse must have the mark of "74A" freeze branded on his left shoulder. If you can't meet these requirements, you can have the horse put down or used in EIA research. These strict rules are enforced on an international level for the protection of healthy horses. The best way to keep your horse safe from EIA is to be sure that the horses he is around all have negative Coggins tests.

Equine influenza

Equine influenza, otherwise known as the flu, is a contagious viral respiratory disease transmitted through contact with infected horses. The virus, similar to the flu strain in humans, often exhibits the same symptoms: high fever, coughing, discharge from the nose and eyes, and loss of appetite. The best way to treat a horse with the flu is to keep him rested, keep him away from other horses, and place him on antibiotics. If only you could give your horse chicken soup! Of course, the best way to prevent the flu is to make sure your horse gets the flu vaccine every six months. After your horse receives his first flu shot, he gets a booster shot one month later and then one every six months. If you plan to travel to shows, consider giving the vaccine every three months. A bad case of the flu could take your horse off the show circuit for several months. Always quarantine new horses for a few days before turning them out with other horses. A flu outbreak can be very dangerous to your horse, so vaccinate and isolate all new horses.

Equine distemper

Another highly contagious disease is strangles, or equine distemper, which weakens the horse's respiratory system. *Streptococcus equi*, the bacterium that causes it, is similar to the streptococcus strain in humans. Equine distemper is transmitted from horse to horse through nasal discharge, poor ventilation, and direct contact. It is very common among young horses due to their immature immune systems. Although humans can't contract strangles, people may be able to infect horses through poor hygiene practices. Always wash your hands with antibacterial soap after handling a horse with strangles, so you don't infect another horse.

Symptoms of the disease include high fever, heavy nasal discharge, and swollen glands that often form pus sacs. Most horses develop a distinct cough and breathing problems. The discharge from their nose is a deep yellow color, and the lymph nodes under their jaw swell. When you suspect strangles, isolate the horse and call a veterinarian as soon as possible. Quarantine all new horses for about a month or until you have them vaccinated. Treatment includes penicillin, drainage by lancing the pus sacs, and continued isolation from other horses. An intranasal vaccine can prevent strangles when given annually or given as a series of injections over a period of four weeks. Your veterinarian will discuss the best option for your horse. Usually, strangles is more of a discomfort and expense than a deadly disease. Again, prevention reduces or eliminates the chance of your horse contracting this disease.

Rhinopneumonitis

"Rhino," as it is commonly known throughout the horse community, is a serious respiratory disease caused by the herpes viruses EHV-1 and EHV-4. The disease is relatively contagious through contact with infected horses, but it can be easily prevented with a vaccine. Symptoms are very similar to the flu. They include fever, shallow coughing, and abnormal discharge. Rhinopneumonitis is particularly dangerous in pregnant mares, causing spontaneous abortions and stillborn foals. You should vaccinate pregnant mares three times during their pregnancy.

Normally, you give vaccinations in the fifth, seventh, and ninth months of gestation in addition to the yearly booster vaccination. The vaccine comes in both live and killed-virus form. Pregnant mares should only receive the killed-virus strain and should not receive the vaccine during the first three months of their pregnancy. Antibiotics, such as penicillin, can help treat any secondary bacterial infections that may occur due to the horse's weakened immune system. In addition, the horse should have plenty of rest and good nutrition. Keep the horse isolated from other horses. As with most viruses, time plays a key role in recovering from rhino.

Equine encephalomyelitis

Known to horse owners as "the sleeping sickness," encephalomyelitis is a very dangerous and contagious viral disease. Usually transmitted through the bite of bloodsucking insects, this disease affects the horse's central nervous system and brain functions. The virus lives in hosts, such as birds and rodents, and is transmitted through mosquito bites. Young horses are the most affected, resulting in high mortality rates. The name "sleeping sickness" comes from the fact that horses with this disease are extremely drowsy. In addition, it often causes partial paralysis. The disease exists in three equine strains: Western, Eastern, and Venezuelan. They all produce the same symptoms and have the same effects on the horse, but they differ in transmission and mortality rate. The Western and Eastern strains are similar in that they are both contracted through the direct bite of a mosquito or horsefly. The Western strain is less deadly than the Eastern strain. The Venezuelan strain is unique in that it can be transmitted from horse to horse. This strain is extremely hardy and can be transmitted through close contact or by an infected mosquito. Although the Venezuelan strain is the most contagious, it is the Eastern strain that is most common and most deadly. Currently, the Venezuelan strain is not in the United States, but since it is common in Mexico and South America, it poses a risk to horses traveling or living in the Southwest.

Typically, the first symptoms appear about five days after the horse is infected. Symptoms include a high fever for one to two days, lack of urination and defecation, reluctance to move, and depression. This disease is fast and furious; death can occur within two to four days of the onset of symptoms. A very low survival rate is common with encephalomyelitis. Horses that do survive the first few days often need rest and intravenous fluids. Most recovering horses suffer some permanent damage, but only a veterinarian can assess the extent of the damage. Yearly vaccinations given before the beginning of the mosquito season can prevent the disease. Initially, the VEWT vaccine, combined with the tetanus vaccine, is given twice a year—once in the spring, with a booster a month later. This gives the horse six to eight months of protection. From then on, an annual vaccine is required.

Tetanus

The anaerobic bacteria, *Clostridium tetani*, cause tetanus or "lockjaw." The same bacteria cause tetanus in humans. The bacteria are usually transmitted through a deep puncture by a disease-contaminated object. Tetanus causes death in 80 percent of the horses that contract it. An unvaccinated horse with a puncture wound infected with the bacteria starts to show symptoms such as stumbling, stiffness, and hypersensitivity to loud noises within seven to ten days following infection. However, some infected horses do not show signs for up to six months.

A distinctive symptom of tetanus is that the horse's third eyelid closes and moves uncontrollably when he is agitated or hears a loud noise. Another significant symptom is the horse's inability to open his mouth to drink or eat. To fight tetanus, you need to treat it quickly. Most horses die when clinically affected by the neurotoxin produced by *C. tetani*. The horse must receive an antitoxin as soon as possible if he has not had a vaccination within a year. He should also receive the tetanus toxoid about a month later. Place the horse in a dark, quiet place and give him muscle relaxants to alleviate the constant muscle contraction. Even after he receives an antitoxin, the horse needs a long rest and constant observation. Have your horse vaccinated yearly and make sure you dispose of rusty objects such as nails, bolts, and scissors.

You can prevent a tetanus infection with an inexpensive vaccination and by keeping your horse's living space safe and clean. Horses should receive the vaccine in stages, usually two to three doses over a period of two months, and then a yearly booster. Vaccinate all pregnant mares at least one month prior to foaling. Foals should not receive the tetanus toxoid until they are three or four months old.

Rabies

Rabies is a viral disease that causes severe inflammation of the brain and is 100 percent fatal in mammals. Usually, it is transmitted through the saliva of an infected carrier. Horses bitten by an infected carrier can start to show symptoms within eight to twelve hours. The first symptoms include excessive drinking, heavy salivation, and disorientation. As the disease progresses, horses can become restless, feverish, and even lose their sight. There is no blood test for rabies, so veterinarians base the diagnosis on symptoms and their prior experience with the disease. The only way to absolutely verify a rabies infection is to inspect the horse's brain after it has been euthanized. Again, the easiest way to prevent a rabies infection is to vaccinate your horse on a yearly basis. Although rabies may not be common in your area, you may want to vaccinate as a precaution. The vaccine is relatively inexpensive and well worth the assurance of a healthy horse.

West Nile virus (WNV)

The newest medical threat to horses is the West Nile virus (WNV). This deadly virus is transmitted through the bite of an infected mosquito. Besides horses, humans and birds have become infected with this virus. Horses who contract WNV show symptoms similar to rabies, equine protazoal myeloencephalitis, and encephalomyelitis: weakness, stiffness, convulsions, and lethargy. If you live in an area infected with WNV, your veterinarian can perform a blood test or obtain spinal fluid to confirm its presence. As with EIA, there is no direct transmission of the virus between horses; the mosquito is the only known source of infection. Therefore, you must control the mosquito population around your horse. Consult your local department of agriculture for information on mosquito elimination and population control methods. This agency can also let you know how many confirmed cases of WNV are in your area. The good news is that many exposed horses never become ill from the WNV, and a new vaccine is available to help prevent infection. Timing is essential when giving this vaccine. To be effective, the horse must receive it in two doses four to eight weeks apart. Both doses should be a month prior to the mosquito season. Talk to your veterinarian about the West Nile virus and find out if it is a real threat in your area. Through mosquito control, limited outdoor time, and vaccination, you may never have to deal with the devastating effects of the West Nile virus.

Equine protazoal myeloencephalitis (EPM)

Equine protazoal myeloencephalitis (EPM) is a debilitating neurological disease caused by the ingestion of the organism *Sarcocystis neurona*, which attacks the horse's nervous system. An understanding of the life cycle of the protozoan helps to protect your horse. The organism uses two animals to complete its life cycle. First, birds eat animals and plants infected with sporocysts, the infective stage of the organism. Opossums eat the infected birds, and the organism begins to reproduce within the new host. These carrier opossums defecate infected feces into pastures, ponds, and feed bins. When the horse eats or drinks contaminated food or water, the sporocysts are easily ingested into their final host. Fortunately, horses cannot transmit the disease to one another, with the possible exception of mare to foal.

Symptoms can become apparent in the first few weeks of infection, or they may take years. Some of the first signs of an EPM infection are a gait that is constantly off, atrophy of facial muscles, and seizures. The progressive symptoms include nerve damage, difficulty walking, general muscle atrophy, and the inability to cross legs in front of one another. If EPM is a possibility, your veterinarian will analyze the horse's blood and spinal fluid to confirm the presence of the infection. No vaccine to prevent EPM exists at present, but medications are available to help treat its effects. Some veterinarians recommend using pyrantel tartrate, a daily pellet wormer, as a possible means of preventing EPM. Pyrantel tartrate seems to have a strong negative effect on the *S. neurona* parasite during certain stages of its life cycle. An antiprotazoal oral paste, ponazuril, has shown favorable results in eliminating *S. neurona* from infected horses. Although ponazuril can kill the protozoan, it cannot repair the damage it causes. Consequently, you need effective diagnosis and timely treatments in controlling EPM and minimizing the damage to your horse's central nervous system. Some other effective treatments include anti-inflammatory drugs such as DMSO, or dimethyl sulfoxide, as well as prescribed nutritional supplements. These therapies are producing a response rate of 60 to 75 percent. The best way to prevent your horse from contracting this disease is through strict pasture cleanliness and opossum control. By raking and rotating your pastures, setting up opossum traps, cleaning your drinking ponds and water bins regularly, and keeping your feed in sealed containers, you can eliminate any chance of your horse coming in contact with infected opossums and their feces.

Botulism

Botulism is quickly becoming more common among the horse population. The resilient and prolific bacterium, *Clostridium botulinum*, produces a toxin that is extremely lethal in small amounts. This toxin attacks the nervous system and disrupts the delivery of neural impulses. Typically it is contracted by ingesting contaminated material or through an open wound. You can find *C. botulinum* in the soil as well as on decomposing plant or animal life. Horses newly infected with botulism have swallowing difficulties, paralysis, and difficulty closing their eyelids. These symptoms usually appear within a week of infection.

Although an antitoxin is available, by the time the first symptoms have appeared, the horse may already be beyond treatment. As the infection progresses, the horse experiences seizures, muscle tremors, and respiratory failure. If given an antitoxin in time, the horse will most likely survive, possibly with some permanent damage. In order to prevent botulism, keep your hay and grazing pastures clean and rotate pastures regularly. As a preventative, you may want to consult with your local agricultural agency about testing your soil for the presence of *Clostridium botulinum*. A series of vaccinations prevents botulism, but you should speak to your veterinarian about the botulism threat in your area. The horse needs to receive the vaccine once a month for three months and then receive a yearly booster.

Lyme disease

Lyme disease is a bacterial disease caused by *Borrelia burgdorferi*. The disease is found worldwide and continues to spread at consistent rates within the horse population. The bite of an infected tick transmits the bacteria to the horse. The risk of disease is highest during tick season, from May to October. The most common carrier is the deer tick, but the bacteria have been found in five other tick species as well. Infected horses become lame, lose their appetite, run a fever, and develop edema. A blood test confirms the presence of antibodies. If your horse has Lyme disease, he should be put on antibiotics immediately. Your veterinarian will decide the type of antibiotic and the length of treatment. The antibiotics usually take effect within three to five days.

To prevent the spread of Lyme disease, control tick populations in your area with insecticides and regularly apply topical sprays with permethrin and pyretherin on your horse. Inspect your horse carefully during grooming. If you find a tick, remove it without leaving the tick's head burrowed in your horse. If you are unsure how to remove a tick, ask your veterinarian to do it. Although no vaccine is currently available for horses, one may be available within the next few years.

Potomac horse fever (PHF)

About twenty-five years ago, horses that lived in the Potomac River area were becoming extremely sick and dying within a short period of time. At first, the sickness was localized to this area, only occurring between spring and fall. Then other cases showed up elsewhere, including Canada, but most of these involved horses that were from the Potomac River area or that went to a show there. The cause of the disease was unknown. Finally, after the death of many horses, researchers were able to determine that ticks and fleas transmitted the disease now called Potomac horse fever (PHF). These insects are carriers of an organism called *Ehrlichia risticii* which causes high fever and other complications. When horses first contract PHF, they may experience loss of appetite, high temperatures, and colic. Within two to three days of the onset of symptoms, horses often refuse to eat and have severe diarrhea; some develop laminitis. These symptoms can last for a week or longer, becoming more serious each day. PHF can be identified with an ELISA blood test that confirms the presence of antibodies. Horses with PHF need to be hospitalized and placed on intravenous fluids to prevent dehydration. Most veterinarians place the horse on heavy antibiotics to knock out the organism. Since the disease has a high rate of relapse, an infected or recovering horse needs be rechecked and placed back on antibiotics if necessary. The best method of preventing Potomac horse fever is practicing strict tick and flea control and vaccinating your horse. The disease is not widespread, but horses that have lived or currently live in an infected area must be tested and vaccinated regularly. If you plan to take or keep your horse in areas where cases of Potomac horse fever have occurred, your horse should receive the initial vaccination, a booster shot a month later, and booster shots every six months.

Ringworm

Many people assume ringworm is some type of parasite or insect because of its name. However, ringworm is a hardy fungus that is contagious through direct and indirect contact. *Trichopyton equinum*, which causes most of equine ringworm, can live on brushes, stall doors, and even in feed bins. Ringworm can spread from man to horse or horse to horse. You should avoid directly touching the fungus that appears on the skin as round, scaly, rimmed lesions. Always wear gloves when inspecting and treating any ringworm lesions. If you are unsure whether your horse has ringworm, your veterinarian can verify this by taking a skin scraping. This is a hard fungus to get rid of because it can often reoccur several times before being eliminated completely. Disinfect all your grooming equipment after each use on an infected horse. It is very easy to reinfect your horse using contaminated brushes and combs after you have cleared up the ringworm.

Rain rot

Another common skin disease is rain rot, or rain scald (*Streptothricosis*). It affects other livestock as well as horses. The organism *Dermatophilus congolensis* lives on the hair and skin of the horse and causes the disorder. The common name, rain rot, comes from the humid and wet conditions in which the organism thrives and the ugly lesions that form on the hair. Because it is highly contagious, you should use a bleach solution to disinfect all grooming equipment and living areas. Keep infected horses separate from all other horses and bathe them with an iodine-based shampoo. Many owners have found putting Listerine® mouthwash on the infected area helps to clear up rain rot. Some veterinarians prescribe antibiotics and advise keeping the horse dry and indoors for an extended period of time.

Noninfectious conditions

Noninfectious conditions can be debilitating and even fatal if not treated. Proper management of your horse's diet, activity, and health can prevent most of them. Like people, some horses are naturally healthier than other horses. Many horses are predisposed to developing certain conditions due to their genetic makeup and to chronic poor health. Since early detection is essential in treating noninfectious conditions, be sure to mention any abnormal behavior or symptoms to your veterinarian.

Allergies

Allergies in horses can become serious conditions. For example, they can cause respiratory difficulties, skin inflammations, and swellings. The first step in treating allergies is determining their source. Some common causes of allergies include pollen, mold, insect bites, foods, chemicals, and other pollutants. You should have your horse evaluated by your veterinarian to determine what the annoying allergens are. Often a simple skin test confirms the reactive allergens. You can easily treat allergies by keeping your horse's living space clean and well ventilated, using steroid therapy, adjusting his diet, and giving allergy shots specifically formulated for your horse. The treatment plan your veterinarian recommends will depend on the severity of your horse's condition. With the rapid increase in the number of allergies affecting horses, many owners are turning to both traditional and alternative medicines to help manage and prevent these allergies.

Azoturia and "tying up"

Changes in a horse's workload with no corresponding adjustment to the content of his feed can cause two metabolic disorders of the muscular system. Azoturia is the more serious of the two conditions. A horse exercised on a regular schedule and fed a diet high in grain to meet his energy requirements can develop azoturia when he stops exercising for a few days but continues to receive the same high-grain diet. When you don't reduce the grain, this sudden change in the horse's work output, from high to none, can lead to a metabolic disaster in a horse not used to such a high-grain diet. The first signs of azoturia develop when the horse resumes exercising, causing muscle stiffening, locking up, and trembling. If not detected, the disorder can lead to immobility as well as severe pain. One of the most obvious indications of azoturia is discolored urine. The urine changes to a deep red then blackish color, caused by the presence of myoglobin, indicating muscle injury. "Tying up" is a similar but milder disorder. This is also called "Monday morning disease," and is caused by the same conditions that cause azoturia. Horses that tie up are usually fed high-grain diets regularly and have a better chance of not developing azoturia. Both conditions are easily preventable by matching the right feed rations to the level of exercise. Be aware of the intensity of work your horse is doing or not doing. Reduce grain intake on days your horse has little or no exercise. Your veterinarian can help you create a balanced diet based on your exercise program.

Anhydrosis

Usually developing over time, anhydrosis is a condition that prevents a horse from being able to sweat. The degeneration of sweat cells and constant high levels of adrenaline cause this inability. Without sweating, the horse has no way to cool off, and the result is often heat stroke or distress. The most obvious symptom of anhydrosis is the absence of sweat either under the saddle or behind the ears after being exercised in warm weather. Other symptoms are excessive sweating when not active, tired behavior, and breathing difficulties. This condition is prevalent in horses living in hot and humid climates and is very common in racehorses. Although there is no cure for anhydrosis, you can treat it and make the horse comfortable. Horses with anhydrosis should live in a cool environment, stay out of the sun, and have a fan running in a well-ventilated stall. Provide potassium chloride or light salt supplements to ease the severity of the condition. If you think your horse suffers from anhydrosis, try to keep him in cool conditions, limit or suspend any intense exercise, take his temperature two or three times a day, and have your veterinarian examine him as soon as possible.

Colic

Colic, or abdominal pain, is the leading cause of death in horses. You wouldn't think a stomach-ache could be that serious, but in horses it can be absolutely deadly. Colic pain leads the horse to roll. This can produce serious twisting in the gut. Of the three types of colic found in horses, the least serious of the three is spasmodic colic. This common irritation of the gastrointestinal (GI) tract can be caused by internal parasites or from eating something rough, such as straw or bark. Usually, only yearlings and weanlings develop spasmodic colic because of their immature GI tract. Flatulent or gastric colic occurs when the horse is unable to release the gas caused by quick fermentation within the GI tract. When the gas is trapped, it puts a great deal of pressure on the horse's large intestine and cecum, causing extreme pain and discomfort. The most serious type of colic is obstructive colic. This occurs when an impaction forms in the large intestine or cecum. An impaction can be caused by severe parasitic infestation, lack of water, ingestion of an abrasive or large object, and overeating.

Early signs of colic include pawing at the floor or ground, constant rolling, restlessness, and abnormal or absent gut sounds. Many horses have an increase in heart rate, blood pressure, and temperature. If you notice any of these symptoms, do not allow your horse to roll on the ground, which is his normal response to the pain. Call your veterinarian immediately. Rolling and thrashing can cause twisting and displacement of the large intestine and cecum. If the gut twists too severely, it could be inoperable, and the horse may have to be euthanized. Surgery can cure some colic caused by impaction, but this is very expensive and not always successful. Walking often relieves some of the pain and pressure caused by colic and prevents your horse from rolling. The best procedure is to keep your horse walking until you can see your veterinarian.

Most veterinarians treat colic pain with flunixin meglumine. Once on the drug, the horse feels less gut pain, which helps reduce his urge to roll. The veterinarian will assess what type of colic your horse has and suggest treatments. In mild cases, these can include the use of an analgesic, flunixin, continuous walking, or a combination of these. More serious cases may require constant pain management, induction of mineral oil into the gastrointestinal tract, IV fluids, and surgery.

Fortunately, colic is a preventable condition typically caused by mismanagement of a horse's diet, feeding schedule, and parasite prevention program. You should feed your horse according to his weight and activity and not overfeed him. If you change his diet, do so over time and not hastily. You must consistently follow a regular and rotating worming schedule to prevent a parasitic infestation in the large intestine, or a severe impaction can result. By creating and following an organized daily management program, you can greatly reduce your horse's chances of developing colic.

Thrush

Thrush is a fairly common hoof disorder that you can easily prevent with daily hoof care. Thrush develops when the frog area of the hoof becomes infected because of exposure to an unclean area, failure to pick out hooves, or infectious organisms. The frog has a horrible smell and a blackish discharge. The pain of a thrush infection causes the horse to refuse to walk and results in lameness. If your horse has thrush, the veterinarian or a certified farrier will have to trim off the infected area of the frog. You'll have to apply an antiseptic solution according to your veterinarian's instructions. Leaving the frog open for exposure to air speeds up the healing process.

Laminitis or founder

Most horses experience laminitis, or founder, at least once in their lifetime. This painful disorder is the result of inflammation and deterioration of the laminae, which attach the coffin bone to the hoof wall. When the laminae become weakened or decayed, the hoof develops poor circulation, resulting in painful pressure. Often this renders the horse unable to stand or walk properly. The cause can be any one of several factors: a high-fat carbohydrate diet, stress, poor shoeing and trimming, and the ingestion of certain toxins. The first true signs of laminitis include the horse's reluctance to move, muscle tremors, and fever. In addition, he tends to lean back into his hind legs to relieve the pressure on his forelegs. Another distinct sign of laminitis is the release of heat from the foot. The hoof feels hot when you touch it. Do not be surprised if your horse resists picking up his foot. Be patient and gentle when lifting and examining the hoof. You must detect and treat laminitis in its earliest stages. If not treated quickly, the laminae can completely separate, which can turn into a chronic condition of lameness. If your horse goes lame, it doesn't automatically mean he has laminitis. Your veterinarian can determine the underlying cause by examining your horse within twenty-four hours of when you first notice the lameness. If caught early enough, you can treat laminitis with rest, proper diet, pain medication, and corrective shoeing and trimming.

Navicular disease

Among horse people, a debate exists about whether navicular is a disease or a group of related degenerative conditions affecting the navicular bone and the surrounding ligaments in the forelegs. The first sign your horse has navicular disease is recurring lameness in the front legs with one of the legs worse than the other. Your horse has trouble standing comfortably on hard, flat surfaces, his stride length decreases, and he may point the affected foot when standing. An experienced farrier may also notice changes in the hoof wall and unusual wearing of the sole. Many factors can cause the development of navicular disease including incorrect trimming, poor foot conformation, and an incomplete diet. Navicular disease has no single cause, and some horses are more prone to developing it than others. Your veterinarian can perform specific tests, such as X rays, nerve blocks, and a flexion test, to detect navicular disease. Treatment consists of proper trimming and shoeing to reduce strain and trauma to the navicular region. Most veterinarians recommend having the horse's heels raised and his toes shortened and rolled. Sometimes corrective shoes, such as bar shoes, can help reduce the pressure and friction on the navicular bone by the deep digital flexor tendon. Your horse might also be put on nonsteroidal anti-inflammatory therapy or anticoagulants. Many owners opt to treat navicular disease with a combination of shoeing, supplements, drug therapies, and alternative medicines.

Internal parasites

Most horse owners agree that controlling parasite populations is a priority in keeping their horses healthy. The definition of a parasite is any organism that lives on or in another organism at the expense of the host. Internal parasites can cause anemia, colic, arterial blockage, respiratory damage, and death. Fortunately, a number of worming drugs are available to assist in parasite control. The following six species of internal parasites are among the most common in horses:

Bloodworms or strongyles

Bloodworms, or large strongyles, are the most serious and damaging nematode parasites. They cause arterial and intestinal damage, blood clots, and aneurysms. The life cycle of the bloodworm is approximately six months. Adult worms lay their eggs in the horse's small intestine, and these eggs are then passed out in the horse's feces. In about two days, the eggs hatch into infective larvae. The larvae spend one week living off the manure and then

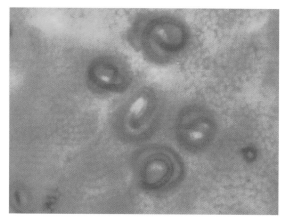

Bloodworms, or large strongyles. Credit: Fort Dodge Animal Health © 2003.

begin their migration up blades of grass. Once the grazing horse eats the infested grass, the larvae start their damaging journey through various organs as they mature into adults. The adult female worms finish their migration in the small intestine where they lay eggs, and the life cycle repeats itself. Symptoms of bloodworm infestation include hind end lameness due to limited blood supply, poor coat condition, and an overall sunken-in appearance.

Threadworms

Small nematodes, such as the threadworm, *Stronglyoides westeri*, affect foals. The eggs are shed into the mare's milk, and the foal is infected through nursing. This infection can cause a condition called foal heat diarrhea. You must clean the foal of diarrhea and make sure the foal is nursing and not running a high fever. You should worm the nursing mare and discuss worming the foal with your veterinarian.

Roundworms or ascarids

Large roundworms, or ascarids, are deadly internal parasites of the nematode family. They are extremely hardy and can live up to a year outside of a host. The adult worm is twelve to fifteen inches in length. This parasite is particularly dangerous to younger horses because

their immature digestive tract is not able to tolerate the large size of the worms. Most adult horses, if not infested, can develop an immunity to them. The roundworm's life cycle is only three months, but their eggs can live in a pasture for almost a year.

Roundworms, or ascarids. Credit: Fort Dodge Animal Health © 2003.

The life cycle begins with a mature female roundworm laying her eggs in the horse's intestine and then the eggs are excreted in the feces. Within two weeks, the eggs become infective and are ingested during grazing. The larvae mature in the stomach wall and move into the bloodstream. As they travel through the bloodstream, they pass through the heart, liver, and lungs. Once in the lungs, the horse coughs them up and swallows them into the small intestine where they mature and produce eggs. While living in the horse, a roundworm infestation can cause severe organ damage, impaction colic, and blood vessel blockage. You must worm your horse on a regular schedule and rake and rotate his grazing pastures. If you have foals or weanlings, it is even more important to keep a clean environment. Worm foals or weanlings every two months.

Stomach worms

Stomach worms are unique because they are both internal and external parasites. Flies are the carrying host of the infective larvae, and horses are the parasitic host. This is the one parasite that requires two hosts to complete its life cycle. First, flies lay their eggs in the infected feces. Within a short period of time, the eggs hatch into fly maggots. The maggots eat the stomach worm eggs, produced within the horse's stomach and passed out in their manure. The ingested eggs hatch inside the fly maggot, and the larvae develop as the maggot matures into an adult fly. The mature fly deposits larvae on or around the horse's lips and on open wounds, resulting in a skin condition known as "summer sores." Once the horse ingests the larvae, they migrate into the stomach where they mature, reproduce, and lay eggs to be passed out. Like most parasites inside the horse, the stomach worm can cause severe stomach damage and disorders, including colic. Because this parasite spends part of its life cycle in the fly and part in the horse, be sure to enforce effective fly control around your horse and his living space by killing off the infective flies. This reduces the threat of stomach worms. Worm your horse on a regular basis and treat any summer sores your horse develops.

Bots

Bots are the larvae of bot flies and they cause extreme stomach damage in the horse. During its seven-to-ten day life span, the female bot fly lays her eggs on the hair of the horse's lower forelegs. One female bot fly can produce up to five hundred eggs; these look like small bunches of yellow granules on the hair. Usually within a week or two, the horse licks off some of the eggs and ingests them. Once they are in the horse's

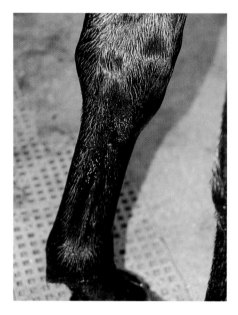

Bot-fly pupae. Credit: Fort Dodge Animal Health © 2003.

Bot-fly eggs attached to the hairs of the horse's lower foreleg.

mouth, the eggs hatch and the larvae burrow into the tongue. From the tongue, the larvae move down the throat and into the stomach, where they attach themselves to the lining of the stomach. The larvae spend eight to ten months in the stomach, maturing into pupae. The greatest damage to the stomach occurs during this time. Often the entrance to the small intestine is blocked. A heavy infestation can result in severe colic. Once they reach the pupal stage, the parasites pass out within manure. If you do not remove the infected manure, the pupae mature in one to two months, and adult bot flies emerge.

Since the bot eggs are external, the flies lay most of their eggs in warm months. The eggs do not usually survive cold weather. To prevent a bot infestation, worm your horse with ivermectin at least twice during your yearly worming schedule. Ivermectin and moxidectin are the only wormers that can kill bot larvae. If your horse has a heavy infestation of bot eggs, you may want to use ivermectin twice in the warm season. Remove the bot eggs manually, using a bot knife. This handy tool has a sharp, razored edge. It removes eggs as you move it down with the natural grain of the hair on the horse's front legs. The eggs are attached to the hair, so you may have to use some force. Be careful not to press too hard against the skin and to keep the blade in a straight downward position to avoid cutting your horse. Spraying fly repellent several times a day on the horse's legs can help reduce the number of eggs laid, but it does not completely stop the process.

Removing the infected manure from your pastures by raking and rotating them is also important. This disrupts the life cycle of the bot fly and reduces the chances of a bot infestation.

Pinworms

Although not as damaging as other internal parasites, pinworms can be irritating, and they are easily transmitted to other horses. The adult pinworms live in the colon where they lay eggs that are passed out in the feces. These eggs can infect an entire pasture or grazing area. Often the adult female pinworm migrates from the colon to the anal area where she lays her eggs externally. These eggs cause such severe itching that the horse rubs his tail against anything to get relief. This in turn causes the eggs to drop and attach themselves to buckets, feed bins, walls, and fences. If another horse ingests these eggs, it becomes infected. Since the pinworm eggs leave the body through manure, you should rake and rotate pastures and remove any remaining manure. If your horse has pinworms, worm him and keep him away from other horses until you have eliminated the pinworms. Your veterinarian can confirm that your horse is free from pinworms through a fecal examination.

Worming your horse

The best way to protect your horse from internal parasites is with an organized and well-planned worming program. Anthelmintics, or

You can purchase most wormers in an oral paste form. Pyrantel tartrate is currently the only wormer available in pellet form.

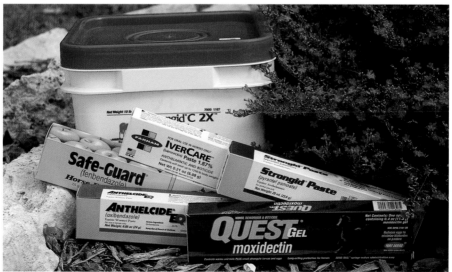

"wormers," are drugs that kill internal parasites by interfering with their neurological systems or starving them to death. Boticide is the term given to those wormers that specifically eradicate bot larvae. Wormers come in an oral paste form and in a pellet form to be fed with grain or administered through a stomach tube by a veterinarian. The wormers are classified by how they eliminate parasites and by their active ingredients. The most commonly used wormers are ivermectin, pyrantel, and fenbendazole. The newest wormer on the market, moxidectin, is showing better results against certain parasites and claiming longer protection than the other wormers.

Ivermectin

Ivermectin is the most popular wormer and boticide because it is reasonably priced and 90 to 100 percent effective against almost all internal parasites. It does not affect tapeworms, which are considered less harmful than the other parasites. Nevertheless, most experts feel that ivermectin provides the best parasite control. The drug works by disrupting the neuromuscular system of the parasites, interfering with their ability to mature, migrate, and reproduce. At the present time, equine parasites have not become immune to ivermectin.

Pyrantel

Both pyrantel pamoate and pyrantel tartrate target the neuromuscular system of the parasite. They are 90 percent effective against tapeworms. Although they can eliminate pinworms, roundworms, and bloodworms, neither is effective against bots. Pyrantel pamoate is the active ingredient in the oral paste; pyrantel tartrate is the only wormer that currently comes in a pellet form. Many owners prefer giving a daily dose of the pellets with their horse's grain for consistent and continuous worming. Recent studies have shown that using the daily pellet wormer may help prevent a horse from developing equine protazoal myeloencephalitis once he has been exposed to the protozoan, *Sarcocystis neurona*.

Fenbendazole

Fenbendazole, part of the benzimidazole drug family, interferes with the nutritional intake of the parasite, basically starving it to death. The wormer effectively controls bloodworms and pinworms, has some effect on roundworms, but has no effect on bots. A recent study showed that fenbendazole was not very effective against controlling small strongyles, and more than half the horses in the study had positive fecal worm-egg counts. Some veterinarians believe that certain parasites have developed a resistance to fenbendazole and that owners should not overuse it in a worming program.

Moxidectin

Moxidectin, another wormer and boticide affecting neuromuscular functions, is very effective in controlling encysted small strongyles and in suppressing the reappearance of worm eggs up to forty-two days longer than ivermectin. It eliminates roundworms, pinworms, bots, and stomach worms, but, like ivermectin, it does not affect tapeworms. You can safely give moxidectin to horses and ponies over four months old. Recently, authorities approved it as a heartworm preventative for dogs.

A worming schedule

Most veterinarians recommend rotating the different kinds of wormers and administering them every two to three months. Rotating the wormers prevents the parasites from becoming immune to them and targets all of the internal parasites that can affect your horse throughout the year. Consider beginning your horse's worming schedule after the last frost, for example, or at the beginning of spring. Plan to worm a minimum of four times a year. However, you can worm up to six times a year. If you are doing a quarterly worming, you can use ivermectin or moxidectin in the first quarter. The next quarter, use pyrantel pamoate. In the third quarter, use ivermectin or moxidectin to knock out the last of the bots. Finally, in the last quarter, you can choose between pyrantel pamoate or fenbendazole. This is just a suggestion. You can decide what wormers to use based on the parasitic populations in your area, and you may want to ask your veterinarian to help you devise a worming schedule. However, plan on using ivermectin or moxidectin at least twice during a quarterly schedule, and three to four times on a bimonthly schedule. All these wormers are completely safe, even for pregnant mares and foals. Moxidectin is the only wormer that should not be given to foals until they are at least four months old.

Safeguard your horse from internal parasites by rotating and raking your pastures. Do not place his feed too close to manure piles, clean his stall daily, and limit the number of horses on one pasture. If you follow these steps and keep a regular worming schedule, you will have protected your horse.

External parasites

Mosquitoes, ticks, flies, mites, and lice are external parasites whose only purpose is to feed on a host and to reproduce. They function as catalysts in many internal parasite life cycles and transmit diseases and other infections. With external parasites, the main concerns have always been the painful bite wounds they inflict when feeding and their role as egg layers in perpetuating internal parasites. However, the real threat they pose is the diseases they transmit when feeding on a horse.

Mosquitoes

Mosquitoes are the most ubiquitous and resourceful of the external parasites. There are over 2,500 species found all over the world. These insects do not limit their host to one species. They feed on horses, dogs, cattle, and, of course, on man. For horse owners, mosquitoes are often more than just a bad bite; they are deadly threats. As carriers of many serious equine diseases, such as EIA, West Nile virus, and encephalomyelitis, one bite can end a horse's life. The female mosquito is the one that feeds on blood from the horse and, in the process, transmits the disease if she is infected. Without this blood meal, she cannot lay her eggs. Once ready, she lays eggs in stagnant water. Most adult mosquitoes only live two to three months, but, within that time, they can feed, infect, and lay thousands of eggs. You can control mosquito populations by removing stagnant water, placing mosquito-eating fish in water troughs or ponds, and using approved pesticides. You need to take these steps in order to protect your horse from the devastating diseases mosquitoes carry.

Flies

Wherever you have manure or decomposing vegetation, you have flies. The most troublesome of the many species of flies are bot flies, face flies, horn flies, horse flies, stable flies, and houseflies. The bot fly lays eggs on the horse's forelegs leading to an internal parasitic infestation. Face flies and horn flies feed off horses up to thirty times a day and only lay their eggs in fresh manure. The horse fly is large, has an extremely painful bite, and is responsible for high blood loss. Horse flies are voracious feeders and are able to move quickly from one host to another, and are known carriers of EIA. The stable fly causes blood loss and weight loss because it is so annoying during feeding. It is a carrier of stomach-worm eggs, EIA, and other livestock diseases. The housefly is by far the most common and numerous of the species. Houseflies are able to lay their eggs in many different places; one female can lay five hundred eggs in her lifetime. Not only are these flies hosts for stomach worms, they also cause "summer sores" by transmitting stomach-worm larvae to open wounds.

To control the fly population around your home and barn, make sure you keep your horse's living space clean and free of manure. Spray or apply fly repellent all over your horse daily or install a fly spray system in your barn. The best kinds of repellents are the ones that contain pyrethrin or permethrin. Remove any dead or decaying plants and vegetables near your horse's living space and make sure your compost or manure piles are far enough away from it. You can also purchase flytraps and baits; even flypaper is better than nothing. As the fly population increases in the summer due to hot and humid conditions, these insects pose an even greater threat to your horse's health.

Mites

Mites, often called mange or itch mites, are microscopic parasites that affect all horses. Mites live on the hair and skin of the horse and feed off its blood. Depending on which one of the four types of mites has infested your horse, the signs may include crusty lesions, hair loss, and small nodules. A veterinarian will have to take a skin scraping to confirm the presence of mites. The mites that impact your horse's health are either from the *Psoroptes* or *Sarcoptes* genus. Mange mites, or psoroptic scab mites, carry out their entire life cycle on their host: hatching, molting, mating, and laying eggs. As the number of mites increases, the horse experiences severe itching and irritation. Soon patches of lesions and scabs become noticeable; eventually, they spread over his entire body. The barn itch mites, or sarcoptic itch mites, are similar to the mange mites in that they also spend their lives entirely on the host, but they differ in how they live on the host. Sarcoptic mites dig deep into the skin, creating tunnels and burrows to lay their eggs. This eventually results in severe skin inflammation, the formation of lesions, and hair loss. The most common type of mange in horses is sarcoptic mange. If you suspect a mite infestation, call your veterinarian for treatment.

Ticks

In the last thirty years, ticks have become more of a problem to man, dogs, and horses. Ticks transmit bacteria and other diseases when feeding on a host. They reproduce rapidly and are very resilient without a constant host. Some of the ticks that prefer horses include the deer tick, winter tick, tropical horse tick, Pacific Coast tick, and the cayenne tick. The main concern with ticks is that they cause a significant amount of blood loss, anemia, and toxic paralysis. Ticks can have one host, or they may require three hosts, depending on the species of tick and their developmental stage. For the species that require three hosts, such as the cayenne and Pacific Coast ticks, the adult stage feeds off the horse. If you ride your horse in tall grasses or if he grazes in them, make sure you look him over carefully. Inspect his ears, abdomen, mane, tail, and between his legs. Since ticks are carriers of Lyme disease and other equine infections, you must remove them as soon as possible. If you are unsure how to remove a tick, have your veterinarian do it. Removing a tick incorrectly could harm your horse.

Lice

Unlike other external parasites, lice are quite host specific. You do not find human lice on horses and vice versa. Lice can live on one host for their entire life cycle and produce countless generations of offspring on the horse. Two species of lice infest the horse: sucking lice and biting lice. The difference between the two is that sucking lice pierce the horse's skin to feed, but biting lice feed on hairs, dead skin, and residue. The irritation caused by lice can be so annoying that the horse bites himself or rubs hard against something for relief. Such actions are constant. Eventually, the horse cuts himself or loses a large amount of hair. In addition to being host specific, lice are very contagious from horse to horse. Lice can live on grooming equipment, stall walls, and doors. If you suspect a lice infestation, have your veterinarian confirm their presence. To get rid of lice, you need to isolate your horse and bathe him with a medicated shampoo for a few weeks. You must also treat all contaminated material and areas with an insecticide.

First-aid treatments

Abrasions

Abrasions are mild wounds that result when a tiny capillary on the top layer of skin breaks. They are usually the result of a fall. Clean off an abrasion with a saline or antiseptic solution, pat it dry, and apply an antiseptic ointment or cream to the area. Leave the wound open for better healing or apply a nonstick bandage to the area until a veterinarian can inspect it.

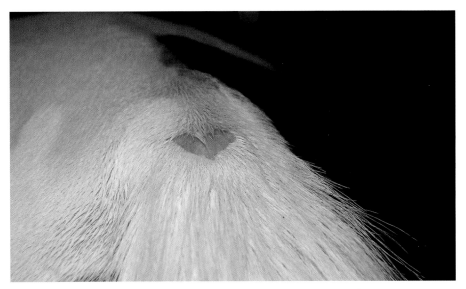

Clean an abrasion thoroughly and leave it uncovered for faster healing.

Bites

The most common bites found on horses are insect bites. Mosquitoes and flies bite horses for blood feedings, often resulting in some swelling. Watch the affected area to be sure an infection doesn't develop. A horse or other animal causes a more serious bite. Horses commonly nip at each other, but sometimes a nip can turn out to be a full, deep bite. Check the wound for teeth marks or puncture marks. As with any wound, clean it with clean water or saline and apply an antiseptic solution. Contact your veterinarian and let him know about the wound. The vet should look at it within twenty-four hours. If your horse is on the receiving end of a bite, determine how bad the bite is and what bit him. A bite from another animal can lead to a bacterial infection or rabies. However, if you suspect a snake has bitten your horse, tell your veterinarian immediately. The vet must administer an antivenin within hours to prevent death. Some veterinarians prescribe an antibiotic as a precaution for any bite wound. Make sure you keep the wound clean and observe your horse carefully until the wound heals completely.

Bruises or contusions

A fall or a kick often produces a bruise, a wound that does not break the skin. Bruises are fairly common and usually don't need any attention, but serious ones can cause severe swelling. To prevent swelling, start by running cold water over the area. Then, switch to a hot compress. After

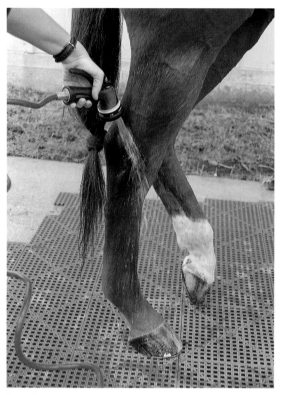

Running cool water over a bruise lessens the risk of severe swelling. If swelling continues for twenty-four hours, contact your veterinarian.

twenty-four hours, use only hot compresses. If swelling occurs immediately, run cold water over the area or apply bagged ice or cold compresses. Do not place the ice pack directly on the skin. Place some rolled cotton around the area, then the ice pack, and then another layer of rolled cotton. You can secure it by wrapping it with self-adhesive bandage. If rolled cotton is not available, use towels or some other kind of heavy cloth. A quilted saddle pad is a perfect substitute for rolled cotton in an emergency. You can also apply a liniment to help reduce the swelling and pain of the bruise. If the swelling continues for twenty-four hours or more, contact your veterinarian because you may also need to give an anti-inflammatory medication.

Bowed tendon

Tearing the deep flexor tendon in the front leg normally causes bowed tendon, so named because the injury produces a bowlike shape in the back of the leg. Limit the horse's movement and hose down the leg with cold water for about twenty minutes. Then, apply some kind of support bandage, such as large cotton padding or quilted leg wraps. Wrap once more with a self-adhering bandage or polo wraps. Your veterinarian should evaluate the injury in order to recommend a treatment plan that may include stall rest, medications, or surgery.

Colic

If your horse is showing signs of severe abdominal pain, such as rolling, pawing, or sweating, take his vital signs and write them down. Listen for gut sounds and look for fresh manure. Walk your horse, stopping only to check for gut sounds. If he is still not passing manure or producing gut sounds within a couple hours and is stressed, wanting to roll or paw, call your veterinarian for further instructions. You should move your horse into a confined area until the veterinarian comes. Be sure to remove any feed. Colic is the number one killer of horses, so you must act immediately.

Choking

Choking can be extremely serious because horses are not able to vomit, and they can often choke on feed. Call your veterinarian immediately. Signs of choking include grunting, extending the head and neck, heavy salivation, and regurgitating feed through the nostrils. Do not allow your horse to drink water because it may enter the lungs and cause further respiratory distress.

Fractures

A bone fracture is one of the most serious of all equine injuries. Some fractures are so severe that they require surgery. Try not to move your horse unless it is absolutely necessary and call your veterinarian immediately. For a leg fracture, you must prevent your horse from moving around or bending his leg. You can make a temporary splint by applying several layers of thick, rolled cotton and a self-adhering bandage.

Eye injuries

If your horse has something in his eye that is causing discomfort or making it difficult to open, you need to contact your veterinarian. Until your vet sees your horse, you can try to inspect the eye for the possible irritant. If you see anything in the eye, try to flush it out by washing it with clean water or saline. Take some cotton gauze or a clean washcloth, wet it in some clean water or saline, and gently cover the eye to keep it moist. When the veterinarian inspects the eye, he or she may stain it to check for any scratches or abrasions to the cornea.

For eye problems, put a clean, damp washcloth or gauze pad over your horse's eye to keep it moist and help flush out any irritants.

Laminitis

Should your horse go lame while riding, you must dismount immediately and contact your veterinarian. Do so as soon as possible because a veterinarian should examine your horse within twenty-four hours to determine whether your horse has suffered an injury or has laminitis. Meanwhile, try to walk your horse slowly to a safe place where he has limited mobility and remove any feed. Check all his hooves for heat. You can also wrap his feet with cool wet towels or soak his feet in a pond or creek for a short period of time. Allowing a horse to stand in cool mud can be soothing for him.

Heatstroke

Some horses suffer from heatstroke if you ride them for long hours in hot weather. You should rest your horse, give him some shade, and make sure he gets plenty of water. Heatstroke symptoms include heavy or strained breathing, excessive sweating, and a temperature of 104 degrees F. Some horses simply collapse or have seizures. If you believe your horse is suffering from heatstroke, take immediate action. Remove all tack from your horse and move him to a cool, shady area. Use a fan if you have one. You can slowly hose him down with cool water or place an ice pack on his head. Start taking his temperature and try to reduce it. You can offer him some cool water to drink, but make sure it's not too cold or it could shock his system. If he continues to appear stressed, call your veterinarian immediately.

Poisoning

The leading cause of poisoning in horses is toxic plants. Your area may have certain plants that are dangerous for horses. Your local agriculture agency can provide a list of the harmful plants, and you can check your pasture for them. In addition, you can request that a local agricultural agent inspect your pastures or you can hire an independent horticulturist to identify any dangerous plants. Having the grass and plants in your pasture identified before turning horses out protects your horse. Because most flowers and ornamental plants are dangerous to horses, you should not plant them close to your horse's living area. Many poisonings occur when owners dump flower and weed clippings into a horse's paddock. Other potential sources of poison include stagnant water, moldy feed, baled hay with toxic plants, and pesticides. Make sure you store water and feed properly and inspect them regularly. You also need to store pesticides and herbicides safely. Do not turn your horse out onto pastures recently treated with them. If you suspect your horse has ingested a poison, call your veterinarian immediately. You can also contact the National Animal Poison Control Center. In the United States, call 1-800-548-2423 or look in your local phone book for additional help lines.

Puncture wounds

Nails, damaged fences, and other sharp objects cause puncture wounds, exposing your horse to infections and excessive blood loss. Treat these wounds quickly and correctly to ensure a successful recovery. First, inspect the wound site. If the object is still in the wound, gently remove it, if possible. If the puncture is deep and bleeding, get a clean cloth and use your hands to apply pressure to the wound. Keep checking the bleeding every thirty seconds. If the bleeding continues for more than fifteen minutes, apply a cotton bandage or gauze and secure it with a self-adhesive bandage. Call your veterinarian immediately. If the bleeding is light or stops, gently pat around the wound with gauze pads soaked in an antiseptic. Use saline or clean warm water to wash the wound of any dirt. If you have a syringe, draw the saline or water up into it, if possible without a needle, and aim the syringe's opening directly into the wound. You can use sterile gauze to wipe in and around the wound carefully. Do not apply a bandage; leave the wound open until a veterinarian has examined it. Your horse may need to be on antibiotics and to receive a tetanus antitoxin to prevent serious infection.

Your horse's first-aid kit

Accidents do happen, so be prepared. Have two first-aid kits handy, one in your barn and one in your trailer or show trunk. You can purchase kits at horse supply stores and through mail order companies. Some owners, however, prefer to create their own kit, so they can choose the size and brands of the materials they need. Whatever option you decide on, make sure the kit includes the following basics:

Thermometer	Vet Wrap® self-adhesive bandages
Nolvasan® cream or ointment	Antiseptic solution (betadine/hydrogen
Saline (.9 percent NaCl solution)	peroxide)
Conforming bandages	Latex gloves
Blunt-edge scissors	Rolled cotton
2" Elastikon® tape	Sterile gauze pads
Syringes (5 cc, 60 cc)	Tefla® "Ouchless" nonstick bandage
Wound powder	1" surgical tape

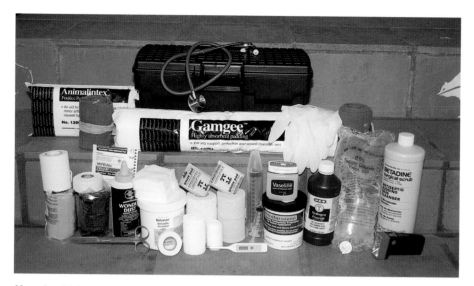

You should have two completely stocked first-aid kits available: one for traveling or shows and another for home use. Many endurance and trail riders find it helpful to carry basic first-aid kits with them.

Stethoscope

Fly repellent

Waterproof carrying case

Poultice pad

Polo wraps

2" or 4" rolled gauze bandages

Petroleum jelly or KY® lubricant

Mini flashlight and batteries

Important phone numbers

Use only clean gauze or cotton pads on a wound.

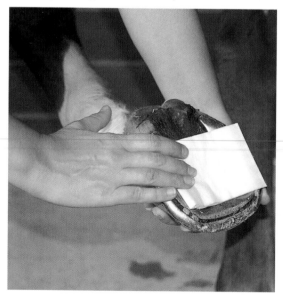

How to bandage a hoof, knee, or hock

If possible, lay out all the necessary materials and supplies before you start bandaging. This makes the process much easier and results in a neater, well-positioned bandage. Also, try to find someone to help you dress the wound or injury. An extra pair of hands is always welcome to hold supplies and hand them to you while you are wrapping the bandages. Make sure your horse is in a clean environment and out of busy areas. Remember to tie your horse using cross-ties or a quick-release knot.

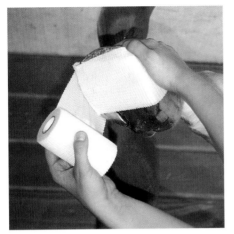

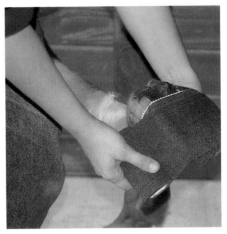

Neatly wrap the roll of elastic adhesive bandaging around and across the entire injured hoof.

Use several layers of self-adhesive bandaging to cover the elastic bandaging completely and to reinforce and protect it.

Bandaging a hoof

- ◆ Make sure you completely clean the wound with an antiseptic.
- ◆ Apply any required medications to the area.
- ◆ Cover the wound with gauze pads or a nonstick bandage.
- ◆ Hold the cotton pad or nonstick bandage in place. Pull an elastic adhesive bandage across and around the pad and hoof several times. Secure the pad to the wound area to prevent it from shifting or falling off.

Be sure the cotton pad or gauze lies flat and firmly against the wound, covering the knee area.

Roll the stretch gauze around the knee area several times so that it secures the gauze pad in place.

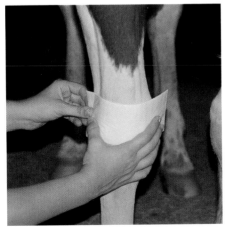

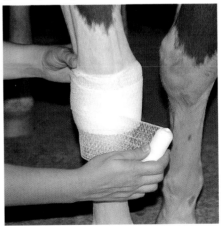

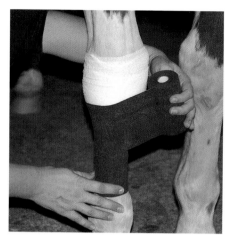

Apply enough layers of self-adhesive bandaging to cover the stretch gauze without restricting knee flexion.

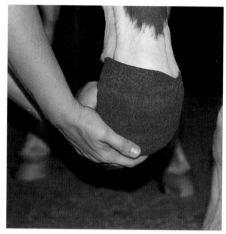

After bandaging the knee, be sure that your horse can bend it. If he can't, the bandage may be too tight, affecting his mobility and circulation; you must redo the bandaging immediately.

◆ Place a final layer of self-adhesive bandaging across the elastic bandaging. Wrap this neatly and consistently around the entire hoof area.

Bandaging a knee

◆ Clean the wound, apply any required topical medication, and cover with gauze pads or a nonstick bandage.
◆ Take rolled stretch gauze or cast padding and wrap two layers of it above the gauze pad or nonstick bandage. Continue to wrap in a consistent motion (you can use a figure-eight pattern) around the knee and wound area until well padded.
◆ Wrap a self-adhesive bandage in the same pattern as the rolled gauze to secure the entire bandage.
◆ Gently bend the knee a few times to be sure the bandage holds and remains secure.

Bandaging a hock

◆ Clean the wound with an antiseptic and apply any required topical medication.
◆ Place a nonstick bandage firmly over the wound.
◆ Using a soft measuring tape or an educated guess, measure the areas between the gaskin and slightly past the point of hock and from right below the point of hock down to the fetlock. Cut the rolled cotton into two sections to fit both these areas in length and

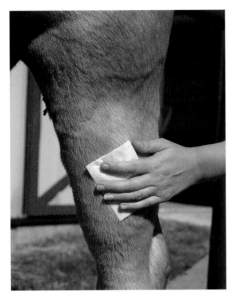

Cover the treated wound with a nonstick bandage.

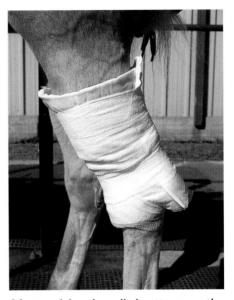

After applying the rolled cotton over the entire upper hind leg, secure it in place by wrapping conform stretch bandaging around it. Do not go over the point of hock. Repeat the same steps on the bottom part of the hind leg.

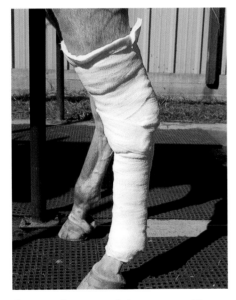

Once you've secured the upper and lower sections to the leg, use additional rolls of stretch bandage to connect the two sections by wrapping them in a figure-eight pattern around the point of hock, creating one complete bandage.

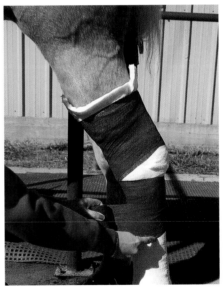

Then cover the entire hock bandage with self-adhesive bandaging in a figure-eight pattern around the point of hock. Wrap enough layers so that none of the white bandaging underneath shows.

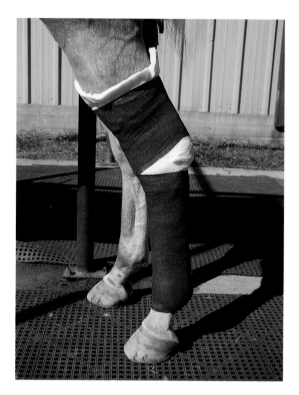

A finished hock bandage.

width. Place the first section of rolled cotton so that it begins at the top of the gaskin and slightly covers the point of hock.

◆ Using a conforming stretch bandage, secure the first section of rolled cotton by firmly wrapping it in a figure-eight pattern. Avoid wrapping the covered "point" of the hock joint.

◆ Place the top of the second section of rolled cotton just under the covered point of hock and situate it around the cannon bone. It should not go past the fetlock.

◆ Using another conforming stretch bandage, secure the second section of rolled cotton by wrapping it in a figure-eight pattern. Remember not to wrap the covered point of hock. Wrap the two sections to create one complete bandage.

◆ Finish by wrapping the entire bandage in a figure-eight pattern with a self-adhesive bandage. Again, do not bandage over the point of hock. Wrap enough self-adhesive bandage until you can't see any of the white rolled cotton or the stretch bandages underneath it.

Poultices

For centuries, poultices have been a natural and effective way to treat sores and inflammations. Many owners use hot poultices to help stimulate circulation around an injured area. The heat produced by a poultice, whether chemical or naturally based, can help speed up healing, assist in wound drainage, and remove any discharge produced by damaged tissue. Cold poultices are useful in reducing swelling, bruising, and muscle strains. You can make poultices from scratch, or you can buy them ready to use. You can use the commercial poultice all over your horse. It is easy to soak in hot or cold water, depending on what you are using it for. For a good homemade cold poultice, boil cabbage leaves for a few minutes. Let them cool before gently wrapping them or holding them to the strained or swollen area. Carefully secure them on the leg or hoof with a self-adhesive bandage. For a hot treatment, you can make a poultice using wheat bread and warm milk. Just soak a slice or two of wheat bread in warm or slightly hot milk for thirty seconds. Make sure it's not too hot; otherwise, it will burn

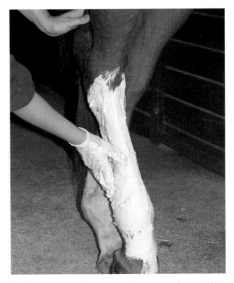

Rub clay poultices gently over the entire injured area using downward strokes. Layer the poultice at least 1/8-inch thick.

After placing rolled cotton over the poultice, secure it in place by wrapping self-adhesive bandaging around it. Don't make it too tight or it will affect blood flow or your horse's ability to place weight on that leg.

Poultices do not need several layers of self-adhesive bandaging, just enough overlay to hold the rolled cotton in place. Most poultices are on for a short period of time and do not require as much protection from contamination as wounds do.

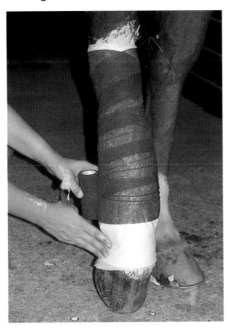

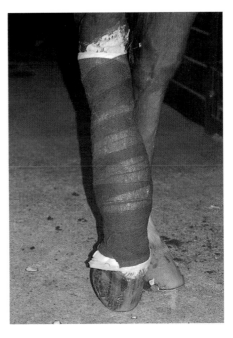

your horse. Place the soaked bread over the injured area and wrap it or hold it gently. Remove it after fifteen minutes. Apply more as needed.

Applying a poultice

- ◆ Thoroughly clean the wound, strain, or injured area.
- ◆ Place the prepared poultice evenly on the injured area.
- ◆ Secure the poultice in place by wrapping one or two layers of wide, rolled cotton bandage.
- ◆ Wrap a self-adhesive bandage around the cotton bandage a few times. Don't wrap it too tightly or it will hinder circulation. Just wrap it well enough to keep it in place.
- ◆ If you are applying a hot poultice, you can cover the cotton bandage with aluminum foil or plastic wrap and then finish with the self-adhesive bandage. This often helps extend the heating effects of the poultice and keeps the injured area insulated. If you're unsure about using a poultice, consult your veterinarian.

Veterinary services

Annual exams

With all the problems your horse can develop, he must have a yearly examination. Typically, an overall health exam includes checking the eyes, heart rate, teeth, and temperature as well as a fecal examination. A veterinarian will look the horse over, making sure there are no abnormal swellings or growths and examining the condition of the skin and coat. Once your horse has received the first series of vaccinations, your veterinarian gives a yearly booster at this visit. You can also ask to have a Coggins blood test done for EIA antibodies. Horse show organizations and boarding facilities usually require a negative Coggins test at least every year. This is a good time to discuss any conditions or behaviors that concern you. Before you go to the vet, write down all your questions, so you won't forget them. Some owners like to have yearly blood tests performed to check the overall health of their horse. Blood tests can indicate if any health conditions or infections need further treatment. The annual exam should be an integral part of your horse's health program.

Pre-purchase exam

Before you commit to buying a horse, have the horse examined by your own veterinarian. A pre-purchase exam is an excellent investment before you buy a new horse. Sellers do not always fully disclose the conditions or illnesses the horse may have had or has now. Before evaluating the horse, a veterinarian will likely ask you how you will use the horse. Based on your plans, the veterinarian may recommend performing specific tests. Usually, the vet conducts a general health exam, checking the eyes, teeth, heart, mouth, glands, and temperature. You should ask the vet to determine the age of the horse by examining its teeth. The vet can also perform a fecal exam to check for worms. To check for lameness and conformation problems, the vet looks at the horse at a stance, at the trot, and at the walk and trot after a flexion test. Some vets want to see the horse do exercises requiring disengagement of his hindquarters and crossing his front legs in front of one another properly. The vet may want to see the horse ridden under saddle. Every veterinarian has his or her own routine and tests to check and confirm the soundness of a horse. Sometimes, the veterinarian may suggest X-rays to eliminate any doubts. Once the health and conformation have been checked thoroughly, the veterinarian gives you an assessment of the horse's overall condition. Most vets won't say, "Buy the horse," or, "Don't buy the horse." Instead, they give you a complete evaluation, leaving the final decision up to you. Although the prepurchase exam may be expensive, it is worth the money to know you are buying a healthy and sound horse.

Dental care

Many veterinarians provide equine dental services; in fact, some specialize in equine dentistry.

Horses have three types of teeth that continue to grow throughout their lifetime: incisors for biting, molars for grinding, and canines (the horse's form of wisdom teeth), which are not useful. The grinding of the horse's jaw shapes and wears down his teeth. Because his upper and lower jaws are not the same size, the teeth closest to the inner cheek become uneven and form sharp edges. These edges can cut into the cheek and tongue, causing painful sores to form and, ultimately, making it too painful for the horse to eat. Using a tool called a float, veterinarians can safely smooth down and remove any sharp points through a process known as "floating." Floats are straight or curved rasps, or files, on long handles. A veterinarian should float an adult horse's teeth at least once a year. Your vet also evaluates the amount of tartar on the teeth, examines the jaw, and looks for any cracked or missing teeth. Depending on what he or she finds, your horse may need to undergo teeth cleaning and oral surgery.

Determining age with a dental exam

During their first five years, all horses lose their temporary incisors and grow permanent ones. A horse's mouth is complete at age five. Between the ages of five and eleven, the cups formed within the incisors vanish in a specific order. At age eleven, the horse has a "smooth" mouth because all of the cups have disappeared. One of the distinct features of a horse's dental development is the formation of a groove on the upper corner incisor known as Galvayne's groove. Typically, it appears when the horse is eleven years old and has a smooth mouth. At about age fifteen, the groove progresses halfway down the incisor. At age twenty, the groove appears down the entire length of the incisor. At age twenty-five, it begins to disappear from the upper half of the incisor. It finally disappears at age thirty. This groove is very helpful in determining the age of older horses.

Maintaining medical records

To stay sane while keeping your horse healthy, you should maintain and organize your horse's medical records. Although your veterinarian keeps the original records, you are entitled to copies for your own use. At a minimum, keep a record of when and what vaccinations your horse has had, a copy of his Coggins test results, and a detailed list of each visit, including the date, the name of the veterinarian, and any procedures performed and medications prescribed. Along with these records of your horse's veterinary care, you may want to create a spreadsheet or use a calendar to note the dates of worming and what wormer you used or will use. Staying on schedule with worming is essential for it to be effective. At the beginning of each year, choose your worming medications, the rotation order, and the dates to give them. Some owners want to be on top of everything and keep updated records of farrier visits, heat cycles, breedings, and purchases for the horse. Maintain your records and keep them in a safe and accessible place. Many owners find it prudent to have a set of these records at home and another set in their trailer or show trunk. Consider buying a portable file folder or file box. A large ring binder with dividers is a great way to store those records and papers. For examples of spreadsheets you may want to use, please see Appendix 4.

Chapter 5

A Well-Groomed Horse

The time you spend grooming your horse is some of the most valuable bonding time you have together. He becomes accustomed to your voice and touch, and while you are grooming him, you can detect skin irritations, swellings, or any other abnormalities. Grooming is very important in stimulating circulation, removing dirt and bacteria, and keeping your horse looking clean.

A basic grooming kit

To do a proper grooming job, you need the right tools. A basic grooming kit usually consists of the following items:

Spiral curry comb and mane and tail comb

The spiral curry comb is ideal for removing hair, mud, and dead skin. Use it with circular and gentle strokes and follow the direction of the hair. You can use the comb to massage your horse as well. Use the mane and tail comb to part and untangle hair. The wide teeth separate hair fairly easily and help to remove knots and burrs.

Soft-bristle brush

This brush removes loose hairs and dirt. You can use it all over your horse's body. It's excellent for removing dust after a ride. If your horse is very sensitive or has thin hair, a soft brush made of horsehair or synthetic fibers is best. Make sure your strokes are smooth but firm.

Face brush

This brush is perfect for grooming the sensitive area of the face because the bristles are usually small and very close together.

Stiff-bristle brush

You should only use this brush to remove dried mud and stiff dirt from the lower legs and the hooves, never on any other part of your horse.

The essential grooming kit should have (*clockwise from left*): a shedding blade, stiff-bristle brush, face brush, mane and tail comb with handle, soft-bristle brush, rubber spiral curry comb, bot knife, and a hoof pick with brush.

The bristles, often made of rice root or synthetic fibers, are usually long, stiff, and evenly spaced.

Hoof pick

This tool has a blunt tip to remove dirt, mud, compacted grass, and stones from your horse's hoof. Unless you pick the hoof clean, bacteria may grow, and extensive damage to the hoof and frog can occur. Some picks come with a bristle brush on the other side of the pick blade to remove excess dirt from the sole and hoof wall.

Shedding blade

During the transitional months when horses begin to shed their winter coats, a shedding blade can be very useful for removing loose hairs. The steel blade is serrated on one side to gently cut and remove thick hairs. The other side is usually smooth and can be used as a sweat scraper.

Bot knife

The jagged teeth of this tool effectively remove bot-fly eggs from the front lower legs. Be careful not to press too hard against the skin when pushing downward to remove the yellow eggs; otherwise, you will cut your horse.

Storing your grooming supplies

Keep grooming tools in a dry and clean place. You can store all of your supplies in a caddy, a trunk, or in a mounted storage bin. Try to keep the equipment away from water and from outdoor areas where dirt and insects cause damage. Clean your grooming tools before you put them away. Many people like to clean their supplies weekly, using mild soap and hot water. You should not share your grooming tools, but if you do, make sure they are thoroughly cleaned before using them on your horse.

A daily grooming routine

Many owners like to groom their horse at approximately the same time every day. Some groom while their horse is eating or has just come in from the pasture. Others enjoy doing it first thing in the morning. What's most important is that you groom your horse in a clean area where you are both comfortable and that you always use clean equipment.

Basic body brushing

◆ Begin by brushing the left side of your horse's body with a spiral curry comb. Do not begin with his face. Using circular motions, start at the neck and move to his withers.

Always start brushing your horse at his neck and crest area, moving down his legs and then toward his hindquarters.

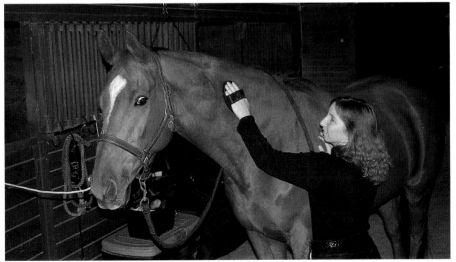

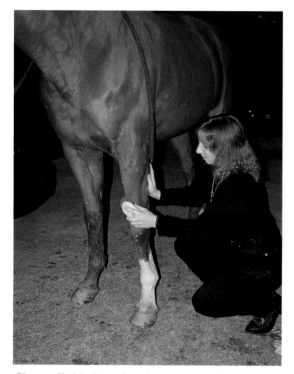

Clean off dried mud and grass around the lower legs with a stiff-bristle brush. Use gentle but firm downward strokes to remove any caked-on debris.

- Work down his shoulder, lifting up dirt, loose hairs, and dead skin.
- Brush across the length of his back, downward across his barrel, and then to his croup, using the spiral curry comb.
- Take a soft-bristle brush and go back over the entire area where you used the spiral curry comb to remove dust, dander, and loose hairs. When brushing with any bristle brush, always follow the direction of the horse's hair, usually to the tail or downward. Don't forget to work the soft brush down his forelegs and hind legs to his hooves.
- Gently brush the underbelly from front to rear, using the soft-bristle brush only.

- Repeat the same steps on the right side of the horse.

If your horse has some mud caked below the knee, use the stiff-bristle brush, in downward strokes only, to remove the tough dirt; work it around the fetlock and pasterns.

Combing the mane and tail

When combing out the mane, start at the forelock and move down the mane. Gently move the comb downward from the hairline. If you encounter any tangles, hold the hair away from the hairline and work the comb firmly through the mane. Using a detangling gel can be very helpful, especially with knots and burrs.

To comb the tail, stand parallel to the horse's hind leg, gently gather the tail, and move it over toward you. With one hand, move the comb from the top to the bottom while the other hand lightly holds the tail. Use straight downward strokes. Remember, never stand directly behind your horse.

The final touch

At the end of a grooming session, some owners like to apply a sheen or conditioning spray, especially if their horse is on the show circuit. During the summer months, a grooming session should end with fly spray, even if the stable has a fly spray system. You can also use a fly mask to protect your horse's eyes and ears.

Apply some fly spray to a sponge and gently rub around the horse's face. Do not use that sponge for anything other than applying fly spray.

Sunscreen is another product used at the end of a grooming session. Light-colored horses or ones with white markings on their face and muzzle can benefit from sunscreen to minimize sunburns and chaffing.

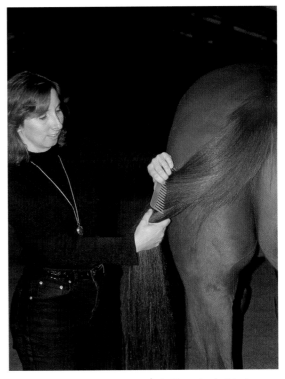

For your safety, never stand directly behind your horse when combing his tail. Instead, stand to one side of his hindquarters and hold his tail toward you while brushing and combing it out.

Fly masks have a mesh netting that helps protect your horse's eyes and ears from flies and mosquitoes without hindering his eyesight or hearing.

If you are planning to braid the tail or just want to keep it clean, use a tail bag while the horse is in his stall or in a trailer.

Cleaning out the hooves

The final step in a grooming session is cleaning out your horse's hooves. This is essential to the care and health of your horse's feet. Picking out your horse's hooves daily greatly reduces the chances of hoof damage and lameness. You must also make sure that you have a farrier trim your horse's hooves regularly.

Cleaning front hooves

To clean the front hooves, start with your horse's left hoof. He should be willing to lift his leg when you touch it or tap it. Move your hand down his leg slowly, gently grasp his pastern, and lift the hoof upward.

Make sure that you hold the hoof firmly with one hand while facing the horse's rear. You can put the pastern between your knees and gently squeeze to hold it in place.

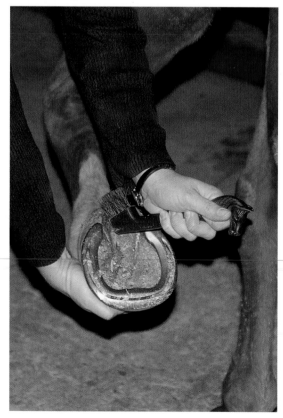

When cleaning your horse's front hooves, hold them very steady and don't lift them up too high, which could cause your horse to lose his balance.

Be careful not to pull the horse's leg to the side. Use the pick to remove compacted dirt and waste from the hoof. Try and follow the natural shape of the hoof to guide you in cleaning the sole. Move around the frog, using the pick to remove dirt that is deep in the grooves.

Once the hoof looks clean, inspect both the hoof wall and the sole for abnormalities or cracks. You can then apply hoof oil, gently release the leg, and place the hoof on the ground. Repeat the same steps for his front right foot.

Cleaning back hooves

Next, work on the left hind hoof. Move your lifting hand down his left hind leg to the fetlock. Pull his hind leg toward you as you face the rear of the horse. Gently rest his leg between your legs. You can easily bring his hind leg over onto your legs.

You can also move his lower hind leg between your legs, gently squeezing the hoof into place.

Use the hoof pick to remove dirt and waste. Brush off all excess dirt.

Gently move the horse's hind leg off or away from you and slowly place it down, rubbing your hand over his lower leg and praising him for his good behavior. Follow the same procedure for the right leg.

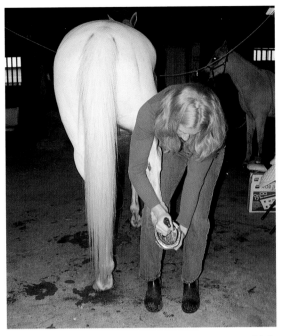

Resting your horse's lower hind leg on your thigh will help ease pressure on your back and correctly position his hoof for cleaning.

General hoof care

Be sure to make hoof care a priority in your horse's grooming regimen. Usually, you should have your horse's hooves trimmed and shaped every six to eight weeks. Horses ridden or shown primarily off grass should be shod. The services of a reliable and experienced farrier are essential to keep your horse's hooves healthy. A good farrier can help you decide whether or not to put on shoes, what type of shoes to use, and how often shoeing is necessary. When choosing a farrier, ask other owners in your area or your veterinarian for a recommendation. An inexperienced farrier can cause your horse discomfort or even lameness.

Regularly trimming the hooves keeps them suitably shaped and leveled. It also keeps the soles and frogs in top condition. The farrier trims the hoof wall to remove any excess growth and then shapes and rasps it (smoothes it out with a file). During this process, he or she removes dead tissue from the frog and sole to keep them healthy and to prevent them from having direct contact with the ground; otherwise, acute hoof disorders could result. Experienced farriers have the skill needed to ensure that your horse's feet are trimmed to the right height and shaped proportionally to his body size and weight.

Horses with leg conformation problems and severe foot disorders,

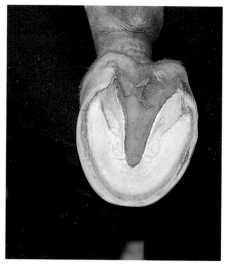

An untrimmed and unhealthy-looking hoof.

A trimmed and filed hoof.

such as laminitis and navicular disease, require corrective trimming and shoeing. Only a certified farrier trained in corrective shoeing can reliably assess the severity of the condition and prescribe the right kind of trimming procedure and the correct therapeutic shoes. Some types of corrective shoes, including rolled toe, bar, and squared toe, can make an impressive difference in improving the health of a horse's feet and his length of stride, allowing gait changes that are free of stumbling or tripping.

A professional tennis player wouldn't wear cleats on the court, yet cleats are appropriate for a soccer player or football player playing on grass. The same principle applies to choosing the right shoes for your horse. Racehorses wear aluminum racing plates designed to be lightweight and to provide exceptional traction on a dirt track. On a muddy track, mud caulks are used. Polo horses are shod with "polo shoes," giving them better traction around tight turns and when making short stops. There are horseshoes to suit all types of horses and riding styles. In addition, general-purpose shoes are available for pleasure and nonsporting horses. Horseshoes come in different sizes and shapes. They are classified as either hot-fitted or cold-fitted shoes. Cold-fitted shoes are the most commonly used since they are ready to use, require no forging or heat treatments, and come plain or with toe and heel caulks for increased traction. Some of the most popular types of cold shoes include the saddle horse and cowboy shoe. Hot-footed shoes are easily

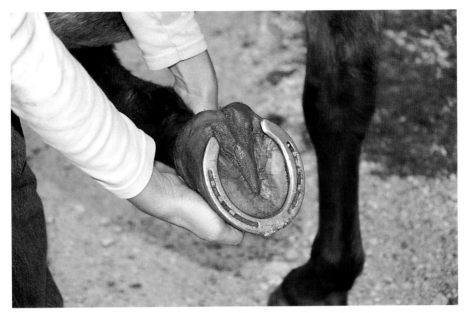

Cold-fitted horseshoes are the most popular type of horseshoe. A horse's hooves should always be neatly trimmed and shaped prior to being shod.

recognizable because they are fitted with extra-long branches. This gives the farrier the ability to shape them to his exact specifications.

Several factors affect the horse's hooves, including weather, bedding, and diet. If you keep your horse's hooves dry, feed him a balanced diet, and have regular farrier visits, you reduce your horse's

In addition to regular farrier visits, you can buy excellent products to strengthen and improve the health of your horse's hooves. Hoof dressing (*left*) can help treat cracking and prevent dryness. Hoof conditioner (*right*) can prevent cracks because it moisturizes the hoof. Its antibacterial properties reduce the occurrence of thrush.

chances of developing white line disease and thrush. You can also keep your horse's hooves in top condition by using topical products such as hoof gel, hoof moisturizer, and a hoof hardener, but check with your farrier first. Applying these products as directed can prevent cracks, retain moisture, and strengthen the hooves. Adding supplements to your horse's diet is another way to keep his hooves healthy. Ask your veterinarian which of the supplements on the market would be best for your horse. Supplements containing biotin, methionine, lysine, and zinc come in powder or pellet form and are easily digestible.

Clipping

Many owners show and train their horses during the winter months in cold climates. Some of these owners use clipping as a method to reduce heavy sweating, which could eventually result in a loss of conditioning. Other owners simply like the clean and sleek look of a clipped horse, which is often eye-catching in the show ring. There are different types of clips: the full clip, hunter clip, trace clip, and blanket clip. Each of these serves a different purpose. The hunter and full clip are the most common. You can easily include clipping as part of your horse's grooming program. You will need clippers and clipper blades. Here are the basic steps in doing a hunter clip:

◆ Find a quiet or low traffic area to clip. Mark out the saddle area with livestock chalk, baby powder, or a washable marker.

◆ Circle or mark areas of the skin that require special attention, such as growths, cuts, and other conditions. Try to avoid these areas, clipping around them instead.

◆ Run the clippers for a little while to get the horse used to the noise. Choose a starting point on the left side of the horse. The middle shoulder or above the elbow are the best places to begin. Work around the head, neck, and withers; move around the saddle outline, clipping the rib cage, croup, stifle, and tail area.

◆ Use upward strokes against the direction of the hair with the clipper blade parallel to your horse's skin. If your horse has loose skin, stretch it with your free hand.

◆ Repeat strokes and start where the last stroke ended. Be consistent and move about the horse slowly. You should have someone help you hold your horse when clipping sensitive areas around the girth and the stifle joint.

◆ Oil the clipper blades every fifteen minutes during the clipping.

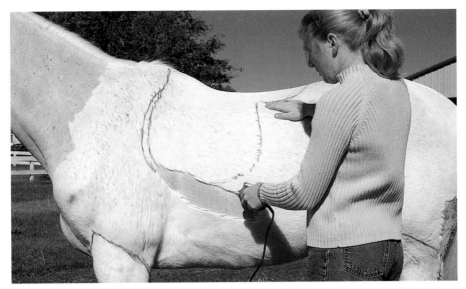

Before starting a hunter clip, use livestock chalk or a washable marker to outline around and above the areas that you don't want clipped.

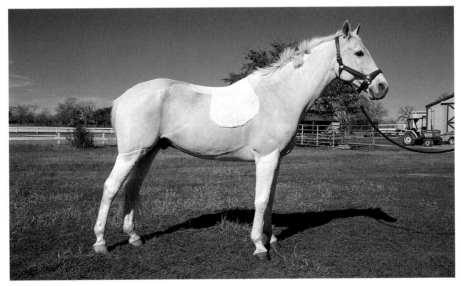

The hunter clip.

You can purchase clipper spray for cleaning as well as cooling off the blade. The blade becomes hot if you use it for a long period of time.

◆ Leave hair on the lower legs and saddle area. When you are finished, have a blanket or sheet ready. You need to blanket a clipped horse when he is outside during winter months.

Depending on the temperature, he may need a blanket even in his stall.

Some clippers are cordless; others require batteries or electricity. Battery clippers permit you to move about your horse freely. They are often the most quiet, an advantage that could make the difference in how well your horse takes to the clipping process. Clipper blades come in different sizes for a lighter or deeper clip. Blades that give a medium cut come in sizes 10 and 15. Finer-cut blades are sizes 30 and 40.

Clean the blades regularly. Store them safely and replace them when they become dull or rusted. Always follow the manufacturer's instructions for use and care. Cleaners and lubricants are available to improve the performance and extend the life of your clippers.

Clipping training: you and your horse

Unless your horse is completely fearless, he will probably not like the noise of clippers. The buzzing noise, especially around the face, causes most horses to jerk and fight the process. Gradually introduce your horse to clippers so he becomes accustomed to their sound.

Have a helper hold your horse. Start by gently running the clippers at a low setting with the blade facing away from him, moving the clippers all over his face and body.

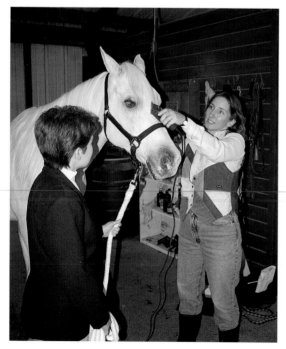

Begin by taking him somewhere quiet after grooming or a workout. Let him smell the clippers. Having a friend hold him would be a big help and be much safer for both of you. Hold the clippers in front of your horse for a time, allowing him to see them. Do this a few times. Then, gently rub them over him. Next, repeat the process, and turn on the clippers while holding them in your hand.

Allow your horse to see and hear the clippers, but keep them at a safe distance. Over the next several days, turn on the clippers and notice how much easier your horse is around them. Assess his reactions. If he seems to accept the noise, turn on the clippers and move them around your horse's body, moving toward his head. If he starts to get nervous, stop and return to that point the next day. Each day move closer to the chin and throatlatch. Most of the clipping will be away from the head area, but your horse needs to be able to stand quietly with the clippers close to his head and ears. This process may take a week or a few weeks; each horse is different. Patience and consistence will pay off. Try not to throw the clippers or shake them in front of or near your horse. If he won't adapt to the clippers after several weeks, you may want to consider using a twitch.

A twitch often helps calm the horse, and he will equate the calmness with clipping. Horses with severe fears of clipping may require veterinary drugs such as xylazine or acepromazine to help them relax before a clipping session. Consult your veterinarian if your horse remains fearful.

As your horse needs to learn how to deal with clippers and their noise, you need to learn how to clip.

Mane pulling

If you'd like to make your horse's mane neat and even, you may want to pull hairs out of his mane. This usually creates a shorter and thinner looking mane. Most owners prefer to pull their horse's mane rather than cut it. Knowing how to pull a mane is very useful if you are planning to braid your horse's mane for shows. You need to use a mane comb, and you may want to use some detangling gel.

- Make sure you comb out the mane fully. You want the mane to be free of tangles and the hairs to lie straight and flat. If your horse's hair won't lie straight or flat, you will have to train it by braiding and wetting it until it does.
- Divide the straightened mane into small sections, starting with the hair closest to the ears.
- In each section, find the longest hairs and hold them with one hand. Use your other hand to comb out any remaining hairs in the section. Do two to three sections, then stop. You can return to the next sections later that day or the next day.
- Pluck the long hairs out at the root as quickly as possible. Pull your fingers downward in a fast and firm stroke.
- Once all sections are complete, the mane should be thinner, and the length should be even.

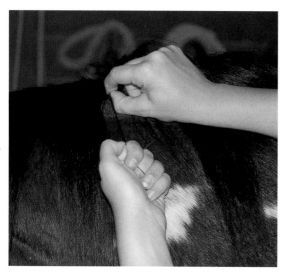

Mane pulling creates a neat and even mane. Because plucking the hairs from their roots is uncomfortable for most horses, work on only a small section of the mane at one time.

Before you pull hairs out of your horse's tail, you should thoroughly comb it so that it is free of tangles. Applying a small amount of detangling gel or conditioner prior to pulling makes it easier to comb the hair and prevents dry hair from becoming too frizzy.

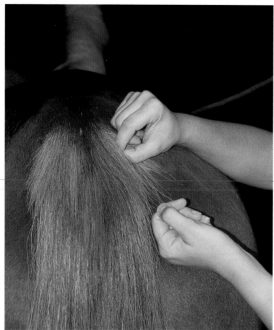

Tail pulling

Before you begin to pull any hair from your horse's tail, you must be sure that you are in a safe position. Don't stand right behind your horse; instead, stand by his stifle and pull his tail toward you. Stand as close to the tail as possible without standing in your horse's kicking zone. Since pulling can cause your horse some discomfort, you should spread out the process over a few days.

◆ Comb or brush out his tail completely, making sure it is free of any tangles. The hairs should be flat and straight.

◆ Grab a small portion of hair, find the longest strands, and pull them away from the remaining hairs.

◆ Pull out the long hairs in a quick downward motion.

◆ Pull out any short, stubby hairs at the base of the tail in order to avoid a frizzy look. To flatten the short hairs, wet them or put gel on them. You can also wrap short hairs with slightly wet tail wraps.

Mane and tail braiding

To get a distinctive and elegant look for a show, you may want to braid your horse's mane and tail. Braiding, or plaiting, is a method of weaving the horse's hair and styling it into a specific design. The result is beautiful braiding that adds definite style to your horse's appearance. Producing neat and even braids takes a lot of practice and patience on your part and on the part of your horse. Before attending any show, check if there are any braiding requirements and restrictions for your class.

Mane braiding

In order to get straight and even braids, you should pull your horse's mane prior to braiding. It is much easier to braid a mane that has been pulled, and the resulting braids are superb. A conditioning shampoo helps to make the mane more manageable. You can also put detangling gel or water on it. Gently comb through the mane and be sure it is completely even and straight.

To braid, you need a mane comb, mane-colored yarn, scissors, small rubber bands, and a thick, blunt needle. You can also purchase a complete braiding kit from an equine supply distributor.

- ◆ Start by separating the mane into equal parts of the same thickness. If your horse has a very long neck and you want it to look shorter, you should plan on thirteen to fifteen braids. If your horse has a short neck and you want it to look longer, you should make fifteen to seventeen braids. The braids should have the same thickness and the same amount of space between them.
- ◆ Begin braiding from the base of the mane, starting at the forelock or poll. Divide each section of hair into three parts and begin braiding.
- ◆ Don't make the braids too tight because this may cause tension and not allow the hair to lie flat. Tie the end of the braid tightly with yarn, leaving some slack for the needle. Firmly pull the end of the braid under, using a thread puller. Thread the needle and move the braid up, securing it into the crest of the mane. Sew through the top of the braid from underneath with two or three stitches.
- ◆ Make a smaller braid, or a "braid button," by rolling the braid into a ball shape and folding it under the full braid. For the best hold, sew through the braid button starting at the underside area closest to the crest and making three or four stitches.

THE ESSENTIALS OF HORSEKEEPING

Using a wearable braiding kit that fastens around your waist makes it easier and faster to create a perfect braid. You can buy braiding kits at any tack shop, or you can put together your own kit by choosing the exact material you want.

◆ Tie off any remaining thread and cut. Check that all the braids are in place and secure. If you're worried about the braids becoming loose or frizzy, you can always use a mild hair spray to set them.

Tail braiding

As with mane braiding, comb out the tail hair and apply some detangling gel or water to make it easier to work with the hair. The tail hair should be long and even, and the hair at the base of the tail should not be short or broken. The finished look of the braiding is similar to a French braid.

Braiding the tail is more intricate than braiding the mane and requires more time. Be sure

Once you've finished the braid, tie yarn on the end of it and run it through the thread puller. This pulls the braid's end up and underneath the body of the braid.

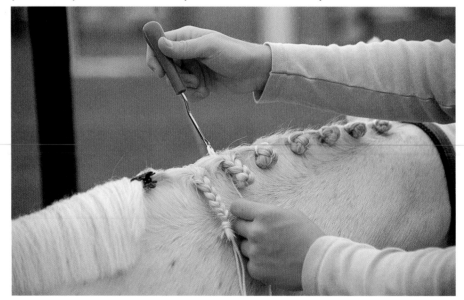

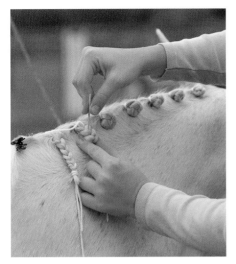

When making a "braid button," sew two or three final stitches through it to anchor it to the crest and secure it in position.

A row of beautiful braid buttons down your horse's crest presents an elegant appearance.

your horse is comfortable with you working on his tail. Unlike pulling, braiding should not cause him any discomfort or pain, which means it is slightly safer to work behind him. However, you should be extremely careful working in that area.

◆ Begin at the top of the tail after you have thoroughly combed it. Start by finding the longest strands of hair from each side of the tail and gently begin braiding them with strands in the center section of the tail.

◆ As you work down, continue to bring in even amounts of hair from the designated sections one over another in order to make the braid.

◆ Continue braiding this way until the hairs begin to thin out or become less even. At this point, gather the remaining hair into three sections and braid it in the usual way. Fold the tail braid under and sew it securely in place. Tie the end with rubber bands or thread.

Remember, getting the braids you want takes practice and patience. Always allow some time during your daily grooming routine to practice braiding your horse's mane and tail; however, don't try to do both in the same grooming session. Your horse needs to become accustomed to

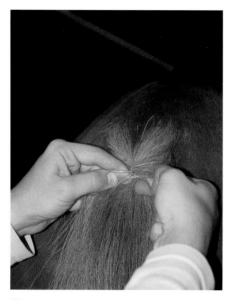

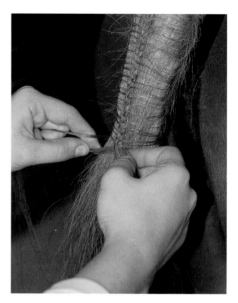

To make an even and taut braid, start as high up on the tail as possible and try to use only the longest strands of hair. Unless your horse has a sufficient amount of long hairs, you may not be able to start or finish the braid.

As you braid down the tail, continue bringing in even amounts of long hairs from each of the three sections. When you get midway down the tail, stop and braid the remaining three sections of hair into a one-strand braid, which can lie flat or be looped up.

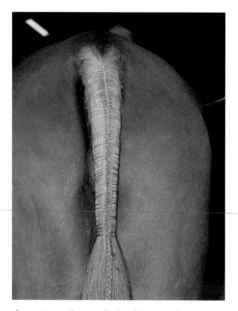

An attractive tail braid on show and sport horses adds a finishing touch and helps keep long tails from interfering with performances.

standing in one place as well as having you work on his mane and tail. Don't wait until two weeks before a show to start practicing. Give yourself plenty of time to learn and to perfect the art of making beautiful braids. You can braid your horse's tail and mane in the comfort of your own barn before you go to the show. Then, you can load your horse into his trailer fully braided. Take your braiding kit and grooming apron with you in case he needs a touchup at the show.

Trimming

Owners with show horses like to embellish their horse's appearance by trimming off excess hairs from the ears, fetlocks, chin, and tail. Trimming hairs from these areas is not required for your horse's health, but may be a requirement of your sport or discipline. In some shows sponsored by breed associations, trimming is discouraged, so make sure you check with them before you begin.

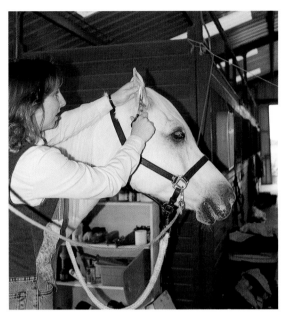

Folding your horse's ears helps you trim the excess hairs along the edges. Never cut the hairs inside the ear because they protect the inner ear.

Ears

Just as when you are clipping, you need to make sure your horse is comfortable having you touch his ears. You should start by gently stroking the ears, massaging up from the base of the ear to the tip. Then, slowly take the ear and squeeze it flat so that the edges touch. You should only trim the excess hairs that cross over the natural edge of the ear. Remember to use grooming scissors with a curved blade. Start at the base of the ear, gently cutting as close to the edge of the ear as possible. Do not cut hairs inside the ear because they protect the inner ear canal.

Fetlocks

Most horses have hair feathering on their fetlocks. In some breeds, mostly in cold-blooded horses such as the Shire and Percheron, feathering is part of the horse's natural appearance. Many owners, who show or who want a cleaner look to their horse's lower legs, choose to trim off the hair around the fetlock and lower leg. Some people use clippers to remove the hair, but many find it safer and just as convenient to use scissors. Before trimming, make sure the feathers are damp and combed out; cut the base hairs as close to the fetlock as possible.

Chin and muzzle area

During the cooler months, hair naturally thickens all over the horse. This is especially true in the chin, jaw, and throatlatch areas. Again, some owners find it safer to trim this area with scissors rather than clippers. Using grooming scissors, find a beginning point by the chin; cut the excess hairs in a straight stroke moving toward the front of the horse, stopping where the whiskers begin. You should never cut the whiskers because they are part of the horse's natural tactile equipment. If you wish to use clippers here, make sure you use a number 15 or 30 clipper blade.

Tail end

Like human hair, the ends of a horse's hairs can become dry, brittle, and unhealthy. Trimming the tail achieves a neat appearance and promotes the growth of healthier hair. Some breeders look down on any sort of tail trimming, so make sure you check with your breed association on tail looks and standards.

First, have someone hold your horse's tail firmly and raise it up slightly. The tail should be combed, free of tangles, and as straight as possible. Run your hand down to the end of the tailbone. Measure about one inch below the end tip of the tailbone; take the hair and cut straight across from one side of the tail to the other. Some people like to braid the portion they are going to cut and save the braid as a keepsake.

Bathing your horse

Bathing your horse is another great way to bond with him. Besides removing dirt, sweat, and bacteria, you also get an opportunity to look him over. Some owners bathe their horse with special dermatological shampoos and conditioners to treat skin conditions and insect bites. Bathing is also a wonderful way to stimulate your horse's circulation and to cool him off during hot weather. You may even want to perform brief sessions of hydrotherapy during bathing time to reduce swelling and to cool tired muscles and tendons. To bathe your horse, you really only need these items pictured below:

- ◆ Bucket
- ◆ Shampoo
- ◆ Scraper
- ◆ Sponge
- ◆ Rubber or soft-bristle brush grooming mitt
- ◆ Sheath cleaner (for stallions or geldings only)

Most bathing kits include (*clockwise from left*): a sheath cleaner, bucket, shampoo, scraper, rubber grooming mitt, soft-bristle brush, grooming mitt, sponge, and hose. A sprayer attachment is optional.

◆ Start by gently applying water to the horse's front left leg to get him used to the temperature of the water. A hose is usually the best way to apply water, but you can use buckets. Next, wet his entire left front quarter from his poll down to where his withers begin.

◆ Don't spray water on your horse's face, especially around his eyes. He won't like it, and he may be spooked by it. Take a clean cloth or sponge and wet his entire face with clean water. Take a soapy sponge and carefully wash around his entire face. Wash off his face with clean water using a cloth or sponge.

◆ Using your soapy sponge or mitt, lather his mane from top to bottom and then downward. Lather well around and down the crest and in the hairline of his mane. Rinse the entire area with clean water, removing all the shampoo.

◆ Lather again down the shoulder and leg to his hoof; massage the sponge in downward strokes pushing the dirt down and off. Rinse with clean water.

◆ Move to his rib cage, back, and underbelly. Wet the area, lather well, and rinse off. Repeat these steps from the hip to tail. Once you have rinsed him off, you should repeat these steps on the other side; remove any excess water with a scraper. Lather his tail thoroughly and rinse it off well.

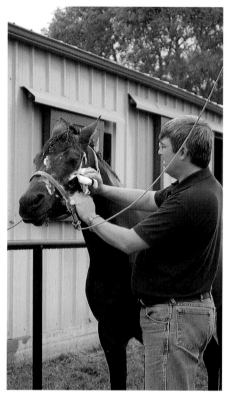

Using a sprayer nozzle is the best way to hose down your horse. The water sprayer should be at a low to medium setting when hosing his entire front quarter. Make every effort not to spray directly into his face or ears.

Wash your horse's face with a soapy washcloth or sponge. Use a separate washcloth or sponge that has been soaking in a bucket of clean warm water to rinse off the shampoo and dirt. Take special care when cleaning and rinsing around the eyes. Pat his face dry with a towel.

◆ Walking your horse in the sun is a good way to dry off some of the excess water. Once the horse is completely dry, many owners like to finish off a bath by spraying the horse with hair polish or conditioner. Always wait until your horse is dry before turning him out to paddock or pasture. Horses like a good roll after a bath, and if they aren't dry, their hairs will absorb dirt and grass.

Hints for bathing in cold weather

Horses and owners agree that bathing in cold weather isn't fun. If your horse gets really dirty during the winter months, a bath may be necessary to avoid knots, hair loss, and skin irritations. Grooming can't always remove the frozen, caked-on mud and stains, no matter how

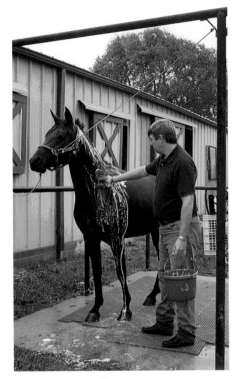

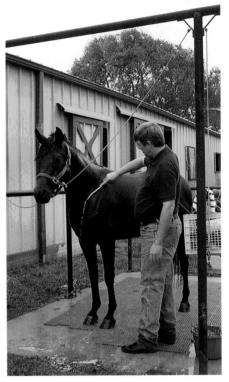

Thoroughly lather the sponge or grooming mitt before washing the front quarter. Pay special attention to the mane and shoulders. Use smooth circular motions to get the shampoo deep into the coat and to give your horse a nice relaxing massage.

When you've entirely rinsed off your horse, use a sweat scraper to help remove the excess water. Use swift downward strokes against his body. The water should just slide off his body and help cut down on the time it takes to dry.

hard you brush and scrub. If you must give your horse a bath in cold weather, try one of these methods:

Take your horse indoors or to a very sunny area and groom him as usual. Work off and loosen as much dirt and mud as possible. Use the curry comb first and then the stiff-bristle brush. Pour three cups of hot water and one and a half cups of witch hazel into a bucket. Add in about nine drops of Lavender or Ylang ylang essential oil. Stir well and dip a sponge or washcloth into the mixture and wring it out. You don't want it to be dripping with the solution. Begin spot washing and rubbing him down only around the dirtiest areas. Don't soak your horse all over. Dry him off well with a clean towel and brush off any remaining dirt.

Waterless shampoos and stain removers can help you spot clean your horse as well. First, groom your horse and check for the worst areas. Apply the shampoo or stain remover to them. A clean hand towel or soft cloth is perfect for working in the solutions and lifting out the dirt. Take another clean towel and dry the area.

Cleaning the sheath

For the gelding or stallion owner, sheath cleaning is one part of grooming that requires a gentle touch and good timing. The best time to clean the sheath is when the horse lets down his penis. This can occur during grooming, bathing, or massaging. Soak some clean paper towels in a bucket of clear warm water. Test the water to be sure it isn't too hot or too cold. Do not put any soap in the water because it could irritate the horse's skin. Be sure your hands are clean. Once the horse lets down his penis, hold the penis and use the towels to gently wash the area. Use downward strokes to remove any smegma. Use the towels only once. Discard them on the floor or ground. Do not put them back into the bucket. With clean hands or while wearing rubber gloves, clean the penis opening with one finger and remove the "bean" of smegma that forms naturally. You can also purchase sheath cleaner at your local feed store.

Only use sheath cleaner or warm, clean water on the sheath. In order to prevent recontamination and possible infection or inflammation, do not reuse the soft paper towels or washcloths you use. Do not throw the used towels or cloths in the bucket. Toss them aside.

Cleaning the vulva

You should only clean the exterior of the mare's genital area, the vulva and labia, if you notice dirt around the area. If that is the case, wash the area to avoid infection. If you see a discharge, however, you should not clean the area because certain vaginal discharges indicate the presence of an infection. Call your veterinarian with any questions.

To clean, have someone hold your horse's tail to the side. You need a bucket of clear warm water with paper towels soaking. Apply warm water from the bucket or hose to the perineal area. Take a wet paper towel and gently wash from the labia out to the cheeks of the mare's buttocks. This moves dirt and bacteria away from the vaginal opening. Always stroke the towels away from the vulva. Once the area seems clean, use clean dry paper towels to pat the entire area dry. Begin at the outer buttocks and move inward to the vaginal opening.

NOTE: If you are planning to breed your mare, make sure you clean the vulva, adding a mild soap to the warm water. Rinse the soapy water off thoroughly, and pat dry with towels. Any excess soap and water could be spermicidal, so rinse and dry the area well.

Chapter 6

Saddle Up: Tack and Horsekeeping Equipment

O nce man domesticated the horse, he put him to use, first driven and then ridden. Since ancient times, man has devised various forms of tack and equipment to assist in restraining and communicating with his horse. At first, bridles and saddles were constructed of the most basic materials, usually whatever was available in a particular area. Cloth, rope, wood, and various metals all found their way into tack.

Today, tack is fabricated out of rugged materials, including strong leather and fiberglass. Because tack and equipment come in so many diverse forms and with so many special features, you may find it difficult to decide what type of saddle, bridle, and bit best serve your needs and your riding style. The following descriptions of the different kinds of riding equipment will help you determine what's best for you and your horse.

Western saddles

The Western saddle is a true descendant of the Spanish and Mexican saddles first used in the New World over four hundred years ago. To control and drive their herds from horseback, cattlemen and cowboys used a working saddle that would later develop into the modern Western style. Its large frame, high cantle, and deep seat make long hours in the saddle tolerable. The horn, connected to the pommel, is perfectly situated for restraining roped cattle and providing a handhold for balance. The large fenders, often beautifully and elaborately decorated in tooled leather, lie on each side of the saddle where the stirrups attach to it and serve as a flat shield between the rider's legs and the horse's body. The latigo, or front tie strap, is slipped through the D-ring or cinch bar found on the front of the saddle. Once tied into place, the latigo is buckled to the cinch and then tightly secured on the other side of the saddle. The sole purpose of the latigo is to anchor the front portion of the saddle onto your horse. Because the Western saddle is such a heavy and large piece of equipment, it may require additional reinforcement on your horse's back end. The flank billet, like the latigo, is put through the back D-ring, buckled to a back cinch, and fastened on the opposite side of the saddle. Back cinches or flank billets are considered optional, but many Western riders find them useful and believe they help maintain a comfortable ride.

One of the most important parts of the Western saddle not easily seen is the "tree." This is the hidden frame underneath the leather covering. Certain sections of a saddletree, including the gullet and bars, define the saddle's shape and dictate how it's meant to sit on your horse's back. Most saddletrees are made of lightweight, metal-wood hybrids or synthetic fiberglass, giving them superior strength and reducing the amount of weight placed on your horse's back and spine. Specific measurements of the gullet and bars help determine which Western saddle design works best with your horse's conformation.

"Rigging" is the specific term used to describe the position of the front cinch ring located on both sides of the saddletree. Saddles are rigged in standard centerfire (basic standard position) or Spanish rigging position, which is ⅝, ¾, and ⅞ forward from the center-fire position. The purpose of moving the front cinch rings forward is to increase the strength of the front cinch and to reduce the constant forward slippage of the saddle. Cowboys who used centerfire-rigged saddles were regularly thrown forward while roping and making short stops as they tried to pen cattle. Saddle makers soon realized that by tightening the front end of the saddle and adding a back cinch, they could substantially reduce the number of incidents of riders being thrown forward and off the saddle. Western saddles come in a variety of riggings, so be sure to ask if it's centerfire or not.

A Western saddle.

You should also ask what type of rigging is the best choice for your style of riding.

As Western horsemanship moved out of the herding corrals and into the show rings, manufacturers redesigned saddles to improve performances within the individual disciplines. The basic Western saddle lacked a horn large enough for the roper, the short skirt for the barrel racer, and a seat deep enough for the reining competitor. Although these schools of Western riding have made considerable changes to the foundation Western saddle, the three principal saddle seats still remain part of their successful designs. The deepest section of the center-balanced seat, used in all-around events, is directly over the horse's center of gravity. The flat seat design places the rider in a central and even-leveled seat, making it a favorite among cutting riders. The backward-slant seat positions the rider deeper into the cantle, behind the horse's center of gravity. Reining competitors can sit in backward-slant saddles with graceful precision, even when hitting those spectacular sliding stops. Manufacturers have created new kinds of saddles with extra features for competitive events including roping, barrel racing, team penning, cutting, endurance riding, reining, and Western pleasure.

English saddles

More than 1,600 years of classical riding and improvements in saddle making have contributed to the development of the modern English saddle. The Assyrian cloth saddle without stirrups and the first tree-framed saddle by the Chinese were significant ancestors in the evolution of the forward-seat saddle. Shaped and contoured to enable the rider to vary his seat position, the original forward-seat saddle helped the rider maintain a forward-leaning position in fast gaits and jumping. Since the early 1900s, the forward seat has been the major influence in the development of twentieth century English riding. It has also been the inspiration for many specialized and distinctive saddle styles. As individual events within the sport and show horse circuit began to flourish, tack had to be modified to meet their specific standards. All-purpose, close-contact, and eventing saddles are all related to the forward-seat saddle.

Early forward-seat saddles were made of only leather and wood. With recent advances in steelwork and an abundance of synthetic materials, riders have a larger selection of well-made saddles from which to choose. The basic framework of the English saddle is its saddletree, which comes in either the rigid or spring form. Typically, most English saddles are made with flexible spring trees constructed of steel and

An English saddle.

wood. The tree should be well padded and paneled with foam or wool for your horse's comfort.

The major parts of the forward-seat saddle are the pommel, cantle, billets and billet flap, skirt, stirrup bars, flaps, D-rings, and stirrup-leather keepers. The pommel is located on the front of the saddle where the two sides meet. The size and height of the cantle, located at the back of the saddle seat, are determined by the particular riding discipline. Large saddle flaps are located on both sides for leg and stirrup placement and for attaching the girth to the billets underneath them. The billets are the three leather straps that harness the girth. They are covered by the billet flap to keep the buckles in place. Billet flaps also act as buffers between the billets and the inside of the saddle flap. The short skirt overlaps with the saddle flap and protects the stirrup bar underneath it. Stirrup leathers with metal irons are attached through the stirrup bar. These are adjusted and buckled to the right length for the rider's leg. The remainder of the stirrup leathers can be secured through two stirrup-leather keepers. Small, metal D-rings are commonly placed on both sides of the pommel, giving the rider the option of using a breastplate.

The all-purpose saddle is a heavier version of the forward seat. It has a deeper seat and padded knee rolls for hunter-jumper events. For the rider at the beginner or intermediate level in both flatwork and over fences, this is the ideal saddle. The advanced rider benefits more by using close-contact and eventing saddles that provide better weight distribution and increased balance. These saddles are shaped to refine the rider's leg position over high fences. Eventing saddles have the deep seat needed in cross-country competitions, whereas close-contact saddles have a wider seat for intensive groundwork. The deeper seat and higher cantle increase back support and balance by keeping the rider's weight toward the rear. The flaps on the dressage saddle were modified to be straighter and longer for improving a rider's leg position.

Many saddle manufacturers are producing an exclusive line of forward-seat saddles in response to the rising popularity of endurance and trail riding among English riders. The big selling point for this saddle is the extra comfort for long hours of riding. Because the saddle is lightweight, gel-padded, and ventilated with a high-tech saddletree, you can ride all day without worrying about your horse's back. Children's saddles are also available for the beginner, young rider, and youngsters involved in various areas of English horsemanship.

Saddle pads

You should never ride a horse without a saddle pad to protect his sensitive back and spine from excessive rubbing and pinching. Every riding discipline has a saddle pad style that fits the length, weight, and purpose of its saddle. Direct contact with a hard, rigid, leather saddle is not comfortable for the horse; and the discomfort is intensified when a rider's weight is added. To understand how your horse may feel, try putting your bare feet into leather shoes that are too small. You'll find it's not very comfortable. Wait until your feet begin to sweat; it feels even worse.

A poor saddle fit can cause painful pinching and muscle atrophy around the spinal column. Saddle pads are frequently used to compensate for this poor fit. Don't rely on a saddle pad to make the saddle fit. Instead, find a saddle that properly and painlessly suits your horse.

English saddle pads come in a variety of materials and styles; however, they are usually either rectangular or contoured. Saddle pads are quilted for better sweat absorbency and to eliminate any slippage; typically, they are made of 100 percent cotton with nylon, polyester, and Velcro® attachments. Dressage and event saddle pads are usually white fleece, but they are also available in velvet or a velvet and fleece blend for superb functionality with show elegance. No matter which saddle pad you select, make sure it protects your horse and reduces slippage. It should also be well made and easy to clean.

Although they differ in style, Western saddle pads serve the same function as their English counterparts. In Western riding, the saddle blanket is considered the original saddle pad. A cowboy would use it while riding and roping, and then he would sleep on it come nightfall. Saddle blankets are typically fashioned out of colorful wool woven into a Native American or Mexican design. Because they are not very thick or absorbent, saddle blankets are best suited to trail and pleasure riding.

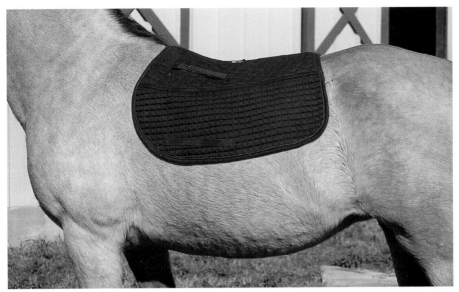

An English-style saddle pad.

The younger generation of Western riders has moved away from saddle blankets, preferring the benefits of using saddle pads. Western saddle pads are filled with felt or wool for thickness, beautifully covered with fleece, wool, or a blended fabric, and adorned with leather wearplates on each side. The large size and long rectangular shape of the plates provide greater protection to the horse's back and spine. Many of the show and competition-quality saddle pads come equipped with material to stop slippage and improve ventilation.

Gel and therapeutic pads are recent additions to the saddle pad family. Since the number of horses with back problems and injuries is on the rise, manufacturers have responded to the need for therapeutic saddle pads. Gel pads filled with a medical-grade viscoelastic polymer reduce friction, distribute weight more evenly, and absorb shocks. Other therapeutic pads gaining in popularity include the double-back fleece and the Air Ride™ saddle pads. Veterinarians are beginning to recommend these kinds of pads in the hope that they'll reduce chronic back pain in horses that are ridden regularly.

Cinches and girths

The saddle would fall right off the horse if it weren't for the reliable cinch or girth holding it in place. Western riders call it a cinch; English riders call it a girth. They are two different names for equipment that performs the same function. Western saddles can have two cinches, one in the front and an optional one in the back; on the other hand, the English saddle uses only a girth in the front.

Usually, the standard Western front cinch is made of thick strands of mohair wool with metal buckles that attach to the latigo and a small leather centerpiece with D-rings. The D-rings on the front cinch assist in keeping a breastplate in place. Back or flank cinches are usually nylon or leather and are always buckled to the flank billet strap. The flank cinch should never be tightly fitted across a horse's underside. Leave a space of about three inches between the flank cinch and the horse's belly. A specialized cinch, known as a roper cinch, is almost identical to the regular Western cinch except it has a wider, diamond-shaped centerpiece.

Cinches are measured in inches and come in even-numbered sizes from twenty-eight to thirty-six inches in length. To obtain the right cinch size, use a soft measuring tape to measure underneath the horse from one side of the saddle to the other. Always add a couple of inches for some extra room.

Girths are made of nylon or leather. They have two elastic straps with buckles on each end and an elongated section that fits underneath the horse's belly. The girth buckles attach to the billets located under the saddle flap. By moving the billet buckles up and down, you can adjust the saddle to a preferred fit. Synthetic girths are gaining in popularity because they're inexpensive, help reduce chaffing, and work just as well as the leather girths. In addition, they are machine washable. Dressage saddles have a distinctive girth, almost like a regular girth, except they have billet keepers that secure the billets in place and allow for a neater, more elegant look. If your horse's skin is very sensitive, consider using a girth cover to lessen the effects of constant rubbing, which can result in

The most commonly used girths and cinches (*from left to right*): leather dressage girth, leather English-style girth, soft English girth, mohair Western cinch, and neoprene Western cinch.

girth sores. Performance and show horse owners usually buy two types of girths: the synthetic for training purposes and the leather to be used only in competitions. On the English saddle, the girth is always placed behind the horse's elbow and strapped across the front of his belly. Girths come in even-numbered sizes ranging from thirty-eight to fifty-six inches in length. Be sure to get the right measurements before buying one. For the horse that has outgrown his girth or is overweight, girth extenders are available to add some length to the existing girth.

Stirrups

Stirrups hold a rider's feet in place while in the saddle, enabling him to stand in the irons and to give cues with his heel and toe. Although they serve the same purpose, the style and design of English and Western stirrups are different.

English-style stirrups, also called "riding irons," are made of stainless or nickel-plated steel. Their smooth, wishbone shape allows ample space for placing riding boots inside, and the flatness of the stirrup foot provides a smooth and well-balanced ride. Small, contoured rubber pads are fitted onto the stirrup foot for increased boot traction and comfort. There are two classes of irons: safety and standard show stirrups. Safety stirrups, which include jointed, foot-free, and Peacock irons are designed to release the rider's foot if he falls off, preventing him from being dragged. Peacock irons are unique stirrups: one side is made of a rubber band and leather loop rather than metal. The rubber band snaps open when the rider's foot hits against it during a fall. Novice riders should always use safety stirrups when schooling or showing in flatwork. Experienced dressage, hunter-jumper, and all-around riders prefer the standard Fillis stirrups or hunt irons. These riders don't want stirrups that can open too easily over a jump or cause a foot to slip out during a dressage test. Irons are sized by their width, from $4\frac{1}{4}$ inches to $5\frac{1}{4}$ inches. They should be about an inch wider than the rider's foot.

The Western stirrup has an entirely different look. It has layers of thick leather to protect the wooden foot pedals from weathering. This padding also increases the overall comfort and support of the feet. Bell-bottom, Visalia, and roper are the most commonly used stirrups. The popular bell-bottom stirrup, found on most Western saddles, has a fairly wide stirrup foot. The sides of this stirrup widen toward the bottom for a cushy fit. The Visalia stirrup is much narrower on the sides and in the width than the others. The roper stirrup is a composite of the Visalia and the bell-bottom, combining narrow stirrup sides with a wide stirrup foot. Safety stirrups have never been a major concern for the die-hard and fearless cowboy, but for novice and young riders, they are a must. Safety-style Western stirrups are not common, although side-step stirrups originally designed to relieve sore and weak knees are equipped with a release mechanism that opens sideways in the event of a fall.

You can easily adjust the stirrup length using stirrup leathers and buckles. On the English saddle, stirrup leathers are attached to the stirrup bar and then buckled at the desired length. Because leather stretches over time, you should switch the stirrup leathers from one side to the other every few months. The most common size for English-style stirrup leathers is one inch wide and fifty-four inches long. Before riding, always check that you have tightly fastened all the buckles and that there are no signs of wear in the leather. A faulty stirrup leather can be extremely dangerous.

Western-style stirrup leathers are actually part of the large fender and are located toward its bottom. Quick-change and Blevins metal buckles have prongs that latch into holes located along the other end of the stirrup leather. To help keep a stirrup in place, the Western saddle has a unique feature called the stirrup-leather keeper. This narrow strip of leather is set above the stirrup and wraps tightly around the stirrup leather.

Bridles and headstalls

Bridles and headstalls enable the rider to have complete control of the horse's head and mouth through leather bands, reins, and a bit. All these important elements work together to communicate the rider's instructions to his horse. English riders call their horse's headgear bridles, and Western riders say headstalls. The major differences between the two styles are that the Western headstall typically lacks a noseband, and a browband is never used on its one-eared, sliding-ear, or shaped-ear crownpieces.

The English-style snaffle bridle consists of a cavesson noseband, throatlatch, browband, crownpiece, two side cheekpieces, reins, and a snaffle bit. These are all connected by small buckles and straps. You can remove each individual piece of the bridle for cleaning or to make alterations. The snaffle bridle, or hunt bridle, is considered appropriate for riders who are at the novice level, who are schooling in intensive flat-work, and who are involved in general pleasure riding. Because the snaffle bridle is so versatile, many riders change certain features as they advance in their training, such as switching to a solid mouth snaffle or adding a flash noseband for heightened control over their horse's mouth and muzzle.

The pelham bridle is slightly more intricate than the snaffle, sporting double reins and the pelham bit. The added reins plus a stronger bit offer the rider refined control over his horse's mouth. In some cases, this is imperative for the right cue to be understood. The advanced weymouth bridle combines two bits into one bridle. A thin snaffle bit, or bradoon, and a curb bit are both secured within the bridle ensemble by cheekpieces and reins. The bradoon bit is meant to sit high in the horse's mouth and apply direct pressure to encourage him to carry his head higher. The curb bit works on indirect pressure from underneath the bradoon, compelling the horse to lower his nose toward his chest. Although this type of bridle successfully expands a rider's vocabulary when conveying specific cues to his horse, it is typically only used for showing in high-level dressage and gaited horse competitions. The hackamore bridle, or the bitless bridle, is used on horses that have difficulty accepting traditional bits. A padded noseband and leather piece are connected underneath the curb groove and then joined to metal shanks attached to a set of reins. Pressure is placed directly on the nose and chin, which teaches the horse to pull his nose under and flex at the poll. Only experienced riders should use the hackamore bridle, since the absence of a bit can affect the rider's ability to stop safely and to handle sharp turns. Hackamores are beneficial when used on younger horses undergoing bit training and for retraining horses with sensitive mouths to transition to a conventional bit.

Because English-style bridles differ in style and craftsmanship, you must get an exact size by following each manufacturer's specifications on crownpieces. Place the end of a soft measuring tape at one corner of your horse's mouth, move it over the poll (where the crownband would lie) and down to the opposite corner of his mouth. Use these measurements when picking out your bridle and remember to look at the size categories.

The typical Western headstall is comprised of a browband, throatlatch, crownpiece, two cheekpieces, a set of reins, and a curb bit. The width of the leather straps around the headstall is a standard ⅝-inch wide. For a simpler headstall, you can use the one-ear or sliding-ear crownpiece instead. Unlike the English bridle, the Western headstall relies primarily on the curb bit acting on the neck and poll. Competitors in high-performance Western events, such as barrel racing and roping, commonly add a noseband to their headstalls for additional control and

The English snaffle bridle and reins.

faster responses. The bosal is a favorite bitless headstall that works on the same principle as the hackamore bridle by applying direct pressure to the nose, chin, and poll. Bosals are made of leather, rope, horsehair, and rawhide. They are secured in place using a fiador (a knot) and a headstall. Most trainers start out using a rigid, rawhide bosal to get the horse's attention and to produce specific reactions. As the horse

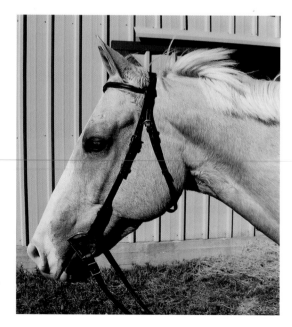

The basic Western headstall with snaffle bit and reins.

improves during his training, they replace the rawhide bosal with a gentler rope or horsehair bosal.

Even though Western headstalls don't come in many different styles, most Western riders own two kinds: one for training and one for showing. The working headstall is usually made of plain leather with rawhide attachments and rust-resistant metalwork for a simple look. In contrast, show headstalls are quite elaborate, boasting antique silver-plated accents, high-quality leather, and hand-braided designs. These headstalls are often sold as part of a show tack set that also includes a breastcollar, reins, and an optional noseband. Whether you are a roper, a reiner, or a Western pleasure rider, you can choose from plenty of fashionable headstalls.

Bits

Bits were devised more than three thousand years ago. The bit has been cited as the tool most instrumental in developing man's relationship to the horse because it gives him direct control over the horse's mouth. Without the use of a bit, a rider (or driver) lacks the ability to effectively, humanely communicate his intentions to his horse. Horses have extremely sensitive mouths. The bit exploits this by applying pressure to eight specific points within or around the mouth: the roof, tongue, bars, lower jaw, chin or curb groove, corners, nose, and poll. These are all key pressure points. Every bit utilizes the tongue, but most operate on a combination of pressure points.

The two basic structures of a bit are the jointed or solid mouthpiece and the cheek rings or shanks to which the reins are attached. Most bits are made of stainless steel, which is solid, rustproof, and easy to clean, but bits are also made of rubber, sweet iron, copper blends, and German silver. Many English riders gravitate toward German silver bits, which are an amalgam of copper, nickel, and brass, because they increase salivation and produce a pleasant taste in the horse's mouth. Regardless of what type of bit you select, make sure it's the right size for your horse's mouth. The wrong size can cause severe pain, resulting in your horse refusing the bit or trying to spit it out, leading to a communication breakdown between you and your horse. Most mouthpieces range in width from $4\frac{1}{2}$ to 6 inches. The Western curb bit has varying cheek sizes in inches in addition to its mouthpiece sizes.

A very wise riding instructor once said, "Bits are only as severe as the rider's grip." The extent to which your horse responds to any bit depends on how skilled and gentle you are with your hands. The complexity of the bit not only increases active control over his mouth but also plays a critical role in synchronizing you into a harmonious pair. As a general rule of thumb, always use the simplest bit. However, certain riding disciplines and horses may require a more elaborate type of bit. The bits discussed below are the principal ones used in English and Western horsemanship.

The most popular bits used by both English and Western riders include (*center, top to bottom*): the kimberwick, curb, full-cheek snaffle, and pelham; a D-ring snaffle (*left*) and a loose-ring snaffle (*right*).

Snaffle

Considered the most versatile and gentlest members of the bit family, snaffle bits are favored for all types of riding styles. The basic snaffle design puts direct pressure on the tongue, bars of the mouth, and cheeks when you pull the reins. Before deciding which type of snaffle to use, consider the different mouthpieces and cheek rings. The quintessential snaffle mouthpiece is jointed or linked in the center. The jointed mouthpiece rests on the bars of the mouth and slightly pinches the horse's tongue, performing what is commonly called the "nutcracker" action. The gentler, solid mouthpiece, known as the mullen-mouth snaffle, distributes pressure much more evenly across the tongue. On the other end of the spectrum, twisted mouthpieces are highly abrasive and, depending on the rider's skill, can actually damage parts of the horse's mouth. The twisted snaffle is a popular bit in Western horsemanship used mostly for training and for getting unresponsive or young horses to pay closer attention to cues and commands. When deciding which snaffle is right for your horse, try to remember this formula: thickness plus smoothness equals gentleness.

The selection of snaffle bits expands when you start to include the size and shape of the cheek ring. The most common snaffle cheek rings include the eggbutt, D-ring, loose ring, and full cheek. These rings affect how well the mouthpiece rests within your horse's mouth, the amount of pinching, and ultimately, how effectively you can steer your horse. The eggbutt is a ring style found on many kinds of snaffles. The overall thick design and smooth-textured joint and sides help prevent pinching around the mouth and keep the mouthpiece in place. D-ring snaffles are slightly larger in size, helping to keep the bit in position and distributing pressure evenly around the sides of the horse's mouth. Young horses and racehorses respond very well under D-rings, but the bit must be situated high in the mouth to prevent the horse from maneuvering his tongue over the mouthpiece. Although the loose-ring snaffle is ideal for horses that have a tendency to lean on the bit too much, its unrestricted mouthpiece is notorious for pinching the corners of the horse's mouth. Full-cheek or Fulmer snaffles have small vertical bars fused into the cheek rings or sides of the mouthpiece. These stabilize the rings in position and help remedy the common steering difficulties many inexperienced riders encounter.

Curb

The curb bit originated back in the thirteenth century with the Byzantines and was later perfected by the classical riding masters of Italy during the Renaissance. After being warmly accepted in Spain's riding schools, the curb bit came to the New World along with Spanish horses. Spanish-Mexican equitation and tack are the foundation of modern Western horsemanship. Furthermore, it was the curb bit that played a key role in the establishment of several Western riding styles.

The curb bit consists of a bar, port, and cheekpieces, which include the purchase and shank. The bar is a solid mouthpiece with a rising center called the port. The higher the port, the greater the amount of pressure put on the tongue and roof of the mouth. Milder bars are normally wider with smaller ports, so when choosing a curb bit, remember that the higher the port, the more severe it becomes. Cheekpieces range from five to eight inches in length and are sectioned into the purchase and the shank. The purchase is the area above the mouthpiece that has substantial influence over the bit's leverage. The shank is the section below the mouthpiece that is ultimately responsible for the degree of leverage administered by the bit and the position of the hands. As those shanks get longer and straighter, pressure and leverage control increase. Curb straps or chains are more commonly used with the weymouth and pelham bits to prevent discomfort and injuries from a medium or high port and from pressure on the chin groove and poll.

By applying indirect pressure on the tongue, corners of the mouth, and poll, curb bits encourage the horse to lower his head, pull in his chin, and flex at the poll. As the rider pulls the reins, the shanks pivot forward putting pressure on the poll, which makes the horse lower his head to the desired level. The rider's grip is a major factor in determining the harshness and severity of the curb bit.

Pelham and kimberwick bits

In the family of bits, the pelham is the parent, and the kimberwick is its child. If asked to describe this bit family in one word, the response would be "control." These complex bits are designed for heightened curb pressure and increased manipulation of important pressure points.

The pelham bit is a merger of the snaffle and curb action in one mouthpiece. It is fitted with a curb chain to intensify the curb action of the bit. Known also as the double-rein pelham bit, it has one set of reins connected to the mouthpiece rings and a second set of reins attached to the shank rings. You can pull these two sets of reins separately or simultaneously, depending on which bit action you need. The pelham mouthpieces come jointed, mullen-mouth solid, or as a curb bar with a port. Novice riders should avoid using the pelham bit until they have sufficient experience using both a snaffle and curb bit separately. Horses outfitted with a pelham must first be well trained and responsive on snaffle and curb bits. Using a pelham on an inexperienced horse could injure his mouth as well as lead to future riding problems.

At first glance, the kimberwick bit looks more like a snaffle than a pelham. Taking a closer look, you'll notice the mouthpiece has a curb bar and port, a curb chain connected to the top rings, and a pair of D-rings for a single set of reins. The port on the bit's mouthpiece determines how much pressure the roof of the mouth receives. The curb and snaffle action of the kimberwick rely on the proper hand position of an accomplished rider, who knows the precise amount of pressure needed on the poll, palate, and corners of the mouth. Therefore, as with the pelham, consult your riding instructor or trainer before transitioning to a kimberwick. Although these bits do increase your control over your horse's mouth, without the right training and experience they can be ineffectual and have long-term negative effects.

Reins

Reins assist you in relating your hand cues through bit pressure and in performing directional changes and halts. As a beginning rider, one of the first things you learn is how to pull on the reins to cue your horse to stop. When you pull the reins, the bit moves into certain positions and distributes pressure to specific parts of the horse's mouth. Imagine the reins as extensions of your arms with your hands at the very ends grasping the rings of the bit. Although your horse's mouth might appear three to four feet away from you, he can feel every tug of the reins as if you were standing right next to him and pulling on the bit with your fingers.

English-style reins are two pieces of leather that are $3/4$ to $5/8$-inch wide and attach to the rings on the bit with straps and buckles. On the opposite ends of the reins, which are four to five feet long, are buckles. When fastened in the center, they form one continuous rein from one side of the bit to the other. Traditionally, reins have been made of dark brown, flat leather, but they also come in raised, laced, or plaited patterns, and they can be made of rubber, cotton web, and rope as well. Some sport and show-event riders prefer the textured plaited or laced reins for a stronger, more solid grip.

Two kinds of reins are commonly used in Western horsemanship: closed reins and open-ended reins. Closed reins are made of smooth leather with a unique end piece called a romal. This long piece of leather is fastened to a metal ring at the midpoint of the reins. The rider gently holds the reins in one hand while the other hand, resting on his thigh, can manipulate the rein length by loosening or tightening the hold on the romal. Many Western riders find that using romal reins improves their balance and reduces constant jerking and misplacement of their hands. Split reins, or open-ended reins, are seven to eight feet long and $3/4$ to $5/8$-inch in width. You can handle these reins separately, or you can tie them together, depending on where you position your hands. Some of the more specialized Western-style reins include roper and barrel-racer reins. Roper reins are actually one unbroken rein designed to be grabbed easily should the rider lose his grip during the high-speed roping event. They are also outfitted with a trigger snap for quick release in the event of an emergency dismount.

Breastcollars and breastplates

For sport and high-performance horses, the girth or cinch is not always enough to keep saddles in place. Painful rubbing and abrasions, caused by an unstable saddle, can result in a dangerous situation for both horse and rider. Breastcollars and breastplates typically made of strong, supple leather, can keep the saddle from sliding back or sideways while riding. On large-withered horses, saddles tend to shift sideways. In Western horsemanship, a breastcollar is used; in English horsemanship, the rider

An English breastplate with a running martingale connected to it.

has the choice of using an English breastcollar or breastgirth and a breastplate, depending on the type of riding.

The main part of the English breastcollar is on the front of the horse's chest. Connecting straps slip onto both sides of the girth and a thin adjustable neck strap holds the collar in place, restricting it from slipping down. The upper portion of the breastplate rests firmly around the horse's neck, and two metal rings and leather straps connect the breastplate to the front of the saddle. The lower portion of the breast-plate goes down the horse's chest between his forelegs and straps onto the girth.

The Western breastcollar is deliberately much thicker and wider than its English sibling. Most Western saddles are longer and heavier and require a heavy-duty harness leather breastcollar to anchor it in place. The Y-shaped, ring-in-the-center design is the most popular breastcollar used in Western equitation. Two wide, contoured leather segments are stitched around a center metal ring. One narrow strap, also connected to the ring, runs between the horse's forelegs and attaches to the front cinch. Breastcollar tags buckle around metal rings positioned on top of the contoured leather segments, and then, depending on the saddle type, are strapped to cinch D-rings or additional D-rings on front of the skirt. The wide leather sections of the breastcollar make perfect "canvases" for leathersmiths to display their

The Western breastcollar crosses the horse's chest and shoulders and is secured to the saddle.

breathtaking artistry. Modified and specialized ring-in-center breast-collars are available for ropers and barrel racers who want additional support and a snugger fit. Decorative and scalloped breastcollars are considered an essential piece of tack when showing in Western pleasure, youth, and theme classes. This tack is more for fashion than function, so be sure to get the breastcollar that best suits your riding needs.

Running and standing martingales

Controlling a horse that constantly tosses his head or that carries his head too high requires the assistance of a martingale. There are two kinds: the standing and the running martingale.

The standing martingale is a long leather strap that slips onto the noseband through a single loop and connects to a neck strap or breast-plate that's secured to the girth. By applying direct pressure on the nose, this type of martingale restricts head movement in horses who tend to throw or toss their heads. When using a standing martingale, a comfortable fit is critical, so keep in mind that you want restriction, not constriction. The Western version of a standing martingale is a tie-down, a single strap with a snap on one end that clips to a bosal or nose-

A running martingale connected through the breastplate.

band headstall and fastens to either the center ring on the breastcollar or the front cinch.

The running martingale, a Y-shaped leather strap, keeps the horse's head low by applying pressure to his mouth. The base of the running martingale must be attached to the girth, and the forked straps with metal rings are pulled forward and connected to a neck strap or breastplate. Reins pass through the rings on the forked straps, intensifying the effects of a rein or directional cue when correctly pulled by the rider. Rubber and leather rein stops keep these rings from moving too far forward. Reins coupled with the running martingale enable an experienced rider to have greater control over the placement of his horse's head.

Both kinds of martingales are available in flat and raised leather and are sized by horse class, such as horse, cob, or pony. Martingales are sold in combination with a breastplate or as individual attachments that can transform a regular breastplate into a functional martingale.

Halters

A halter is basically an English bridle minus the browband, bit, and reins and with an added strap that goes under the jaw. Since most horses are led and handled with a halter throughout their lives, early training is essential to their accepting it. Nylon halters seem to be the most popular because they are inexpensive, durable, easy to clean, and lightweight. Leather halters have the elegant look of a bridle, but, unfortunately, they require more cleaning and upkeep than their nylon counterparts. Many owners use a leather halter only at shows to add to their horse's refined look. All halters are equipped with small brass rings and hardware that conjoin the bands and are used for clipping lead rope or cross-tie snaps onto them. The large buckle on the crownband permits easy adjustments to the halter's fit and keeps the halter firmly in place.

The halter should not be too tight around the horse's head; it should be just snug enough so that it can't slip off when pulled.

As your horse matures, make sure his halter grows with him. Putting an adult-sized halter on a small foal is asking for trouble. Typical halter sizes include foal, yearling, small, and average. Customized halters are available for cobs, ponies, and draft horses. The breakaway halter is great for training green horses how to be handled on a lead rope and how to stand still while being tied. If a scared horse pulls back or spooks in a tied halter, he could seriously hurt himself. Using the breakaway halter helps prevent injuries because it snaps open when pressure is applied to certain halter bands. It's easy to find a wide selection of halters in a rainbow of colors and premium leathers. Many owners like to personalize the halter by having their horse's name on a brass nameplate or embroidered on the noseband or cheekband.

Blankets and sheets

So many types of blankets and sheets are on the market that it's often difficult to distinguish among them. To make it a little easier, think of blankets as heavy coats and sheets as light jackets that are used to keep your horse warm, clean, and dry. Most blankets and sheets cover a horse from his withers to his tailhead and extend to just above his forearms and gaskins. Standard features on all blankets and sheets guarantee a proper fit by means of adjustable leg straps, surcingles with straps that cross underneath or tightly around the barrel, tail flaps, and two-buckle chest closures.

Stable blankets

Stable blankets keep your horse warm when he is in his stall or the barn. Typically, these blankets are quilted and insulated with fiberfill. The outer shell is made of nylon or polyester. The thickness of the blanket is measured in deniers, which many manufacturers include as part of their product's name or description. Most stable blankets have a bulk measurement of between 600 deniers (low) and 1,200 deniers (high). Strictly speaking, a stable blanket should only be used when a horse is indoors since it is not made to withstand long periods of wet weather, high winds, or cold temperatures. For additional warmth on cold nights in the barn, you can place a blanket liner underneath the stable blanket. Just make sure your horse doesn't become overheated.

Turnout blankets

Constructed to take all of Mother Nature's wrath, turnout blankets are perfect for the horse that spends most of his time outdoors, especially during periods of rain, snow, high winds, and cold temperatures. These

A turnout blanket provides protection for horses out for long hours in inclement weather. Determine your horse's exact measurements for a perfect fit.

durable blankets have a waterproof and breathable outer shell made of nylon, Teflon®, or polyester combined with exceptionally warm fiber-fill insulation. Turnout blankets are made with movement and shifting in mind and are fitted with T-shaped buckles on the chest closure for a secure fit. Many owners add an insulated hood for neck and face protection. Always check the blanket's fit at least once a day to be sure it's not falling off or rubbing too much. Wash the turnout blanket after your horse has worn it a few of times or if it gets very dirty. This prevents a buildup of bacteria, dirt, and yeast that could develop into skin irritations and fungal conditions. It's always a good idea to have two turnout blankets so you can alternate them.

Sheets

Sheets offer lighter protection than blankets and come in an assortment of styles: dress, three-season, summer, anti-sweat, fly, and exercise. Each type serves a particular function. Sheets are fabricated out of a combination of synthetic materials. Unlike blankets, sheets are meant for milder weather and for use over shorter periods of time. They are, however, practically identical to the blanket in body shape and design.

A dress sheet is perfect for keeping show horses clean after you bathe and clip them. The fleece material, which has a luxuriously soft appearance, keeps the horse warm and dry. Many owners and breeders have their dress sheets customized with their name, logo, or the name of their horse or stable. The three-season sheets are perfect for short turnout periods during the fall, winter, and spring. Waterproof, breathable, and made of nylon, these sheets are best for milder temperatures. They give excellent protection from light rain, snow, and wind. Summer sheets are made for those staggeringly hot days out on pasture. Fashioned to be lightweight and strong, they have a mesh or cotton lining. This sheet keeps your horse cool throughout the day and prevents sunburn. Consider using a summer sheet if your horse spends long periods of time outdoors. You'll also want to use it during peak hours of sunlight.

After a hard workout your horse needs to cool down. His sweat must dry completely to avoid getting a chill. Anti-sweat sheets, which come in a woven mesh pattern, provide exceptional ventilation for fast evaporation without a significant drop in body temperature.

Fly sheets are basically an expanded version of the fly mask. The nylon mesh construction offers light and airy protection from annoying and risky insect bites. Because it's so similar to the summer sheet, owners tend to use only a fly sheet during the summer months.

The exercise sheet keeps a clipped horse warm while being ridden in cool weather. It has a slightly different look from the other sheets. There is no material over the shoulders and forearms, allowing the horse unrestricted movement in his forequarters. Unlike blankets and other sheets, the exercise sheet covers the entire back and hindquarters, reaching down only to the elbows and stifles. The blanket clip is done specifically for this type of sheet with the addition of another blanket in mind.

Exercise and shipping boots

You can protect athletic and high-performance horses from injuring their feet and lower legs with exercise boots. Bell, splint, ankle, and Sports Medicine™ boots are available to provide extra support around specific areas of the horse's lower legs. At one time, exercise boots were only put on the forelegs, but recently, many trainers have found that putting certain types on all legs can provide more protection and improve performance. Shipping boots offer increased support and cushioning around the lower legs when the horse is in a trailer or is being transported. Experts recommend that you only use exercise boots when you are riding your horse. You should not use them when you are shipping him.

Bell boots, available in rubber, PVC, and nylon hybrids, are bell-shaped to fit over the complete hoof area. They are flexible, providing full or partial protection. You should always use bell boots for cross-country and hunter-jumper event horses to prevent cracking or bruising if their hooves knock into a pole or fence. Gaited horses and horses prone to overreaching their hind feet to their forelegs need bell boots to prevent heel and toe injuries.

Splint boots help support and protect the splint and sesamoid bones. Because these boots fit from below the knee or hock down to the fetlock, they protect the lower legs from the excessive force active horses place on them. Velcro® straps on neoprene and Kevlar® boots fasten protective suede padding into place, minimizing any brushing between the forelegs.

Ankle boots, similar to splint boots, are a requirement for high-performance horses at risk of injuring their ankles and in need of reinforcement around their unprotected fetlock joints. Sport Medicine Boots ™ are the most recent addition to the exercise boot collection. They were created as a result of extensive research carried out in equine physiology and sports medicine. Durable, made of neoprene for flexi-

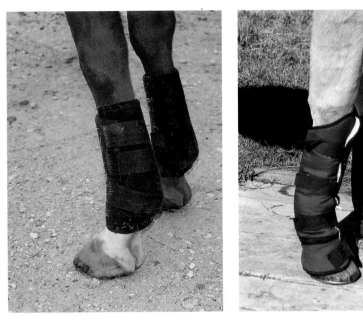

Exercise boots, a requirement for active and sport performance horses, provide excellent support and reinforcement to the lower legs. Velcro® straps make it easy to adjust the boots to the width and height needed.

Shipping boots protect the lower legs from bruising and serious injury while you are transporting your horse. Properly applied, the shipping boots cover the hoof wall area just above the toe and up to the knee.

bility and weathering, these boots absorb heavy shocks and trauma to the fetlocks, splints, and feet. Sport Medicine Boots™ are a wise investment for the active and athletic horse and for pleasure horses, young horses, and older horses prone to lower leg injuries due to weak and underdeveloped tendons and ligaments.

Shipping boots pad the horse's lower legs and protect them when traveling. A horse often kicks or knocks his legs into the sides of trailers and shipping stalls, causing serious bruising and injuries. Placing the foam-filled boots around each lower leg reduces the chances of this happening. The front boots cover the hoof up to the knee, and the hind boots offer slightly more leg protection from just above the hock down to the coronet. They are lined with fleece for comfort and are waterproof. The boots wrap around the legs using four to five Velcro straps for a tight fit. A four-boot set is an essential piece of equipment for any owner considering traveling with or shipping his horse. Allow your horse time to become accustomed to the strange heaviness of the boots around his legs by putting them on him for an hour every day until he seems completely at ease with them. Don't wait until the day you need to trailer or ship him to put them on for the first time.

Cleaning and storing tack

Reliable, strong, contoured, and elegant are just a few of the words that describe the beauty and benefits of using leather tack. However, in order to keep your tack shining and in top condition, you must clean it and store it correctly. Excessive exposure to dirt, bacteria, and mold can easily damage leather, making your tack unsafe and unattractive. Cleaning the saddle, bridle, reins, and girth does not have to be a weekly chore. The best idea is to clean as you go, only doing a complete cleaning session when dirt has begun to build up and cracks have become fairly obvious. After every ride, try to wipe down all your tack thoroughly with a damp, warm cloth. Give it time to dry and put it in a clean tack room or in saddle and bridle bags. Inexpensive saddle covers provide excellent protection against dust, water, and abrasions, and they add years to the life of your saddle. Strict storage techniques and wiping your tack down regularly should drastically cut the time it takes to clean and condition it.

Tack cleaning is a rainy-day chore for most riders. If you can't be out riding, stay in the barn and clean your tack. Find a quiet spot and a stool to sit on; be sure you have all of your supplies before you begin. A complete tack cleaning kit should include the following:

- ◆ Leather cleaner or saddle soap
- ◆ Leather conditioner or oil
- ◆ Clean, cotton hand towels or rags and a polishing cloth
- ◆ Sponge
- ◆ Metal polish
- ◆ Eraser (optional)
- ◆ Soft toothbrush
- ◆ Bucket with clean, warm water

Although the tack cleaning method described here is for English leather tack, the instructions are applicable to other leather tack.

Cleaning the bridle and reins
- ◆ Take the bridle or reins apart and lay out the leather strips. Soak the bit in a bucket of clean, warm water. The water should help loosen any caked grass. Work a toothbrush over the entire bit, especially around the joint and rings.

◆ Clean all metal work with metal polish and a polishing cloth. Avoid spraying or rubbing the metal polish onto the leather.

◆ Take a damp sponge and add soap or leather cleaner to it. After working up a lather, begin moving the soapy sponge in circular motions up and down the leather piece and from front to back.

◆ Using the toothbrush, go over the area you worked on with the sponge, paying close attention to areas with plaiting or cracks.

◆ Dry the leather with a clean cloth and hang it or lay it out on a clean towel while working on another piece. Once all the tack is dry, apply the leather conditioner.

◆ Remove the bit from the soaking bucket. Dry the bit with a towel and buff it to a nice shine with an eraser and a clean cloth.

◆ Reassemble the bridle and reins for proper storage.

Cleaning the saddle

◆ Place the saddle either on a saddle stand or a sawhorse. This makes it much easier to clean. Remove the stirrup leathers, girth, and billet flaps; clean and condition them exactly as you did the leather bands on the bridle. Soak the metal stirrups in warm water to loosen any caked mud or grass and polish them.

◆ Put cleaner or soap on a damp, clean cloth or sponge and begin gently wiping the underside of the saddle. Pay special attention to the panels and sweat flaps. Dry the underneath of the saddle with a clean cloth before moving to the topside of the saddle.

◆ Wipe the entire seat and flaps with a plain damp cloth. Using circular motions, rub a damp sponge or cloth with soap or cleaner all around the seat, between the flaps, and over the panels. Remove any excess soap or cleaner to avoid film residue and let dry.

◆ Apply conditioner or oil once the saddle is dry. Use a clean cloth or small paintbrush. After the conditioner or oil has soaked in, put the saddle together.

Getting the right fit

Riding in poorly fitted or incorrectly sized tack affects performance, and it can also cause dangerous accidents and painful injuries. Therefore, take steps to ensure that you use only comfortable and safe tack when riding your horse. With the large selection of saddles available, you should be able to find one that fits your horse flawlessly and comfortably. By extending and tightening the leather straps, you can easily adjust the bridle and bit positions, but because saddle fits are slightly harder to correct, you should try a saddle on your horse before you buy it. Most reputable tack stores and mail-order companies recommend that you do this, and they are happy to lend you their sample models to help you decide which saddle best suits your horse's conformation. If they don't, go somewhere where they will. The tack store or mail-order company that isn't concerned with saddle fit is not concerned about your horse's comfort and back. Blankets and sheets also need to be measured to fit.

Fitting a saddle

As a courtesy to the tack store, always bathe and groom your horse before you start a saddle fashion show on your horse's back. First, make sure he is dry. Then, without a saddle pad, place the saddle slightly forward on his back and move it back to where the pommel rests above his withers. Position it to where the girth would lie, approximately four inches from the elbow, but do not attach the girth yet.

Next, look at the back end of the saddle on your horse's back. It should sit flat and not tilt forward or backward. The saddletree should not sit so low that it touches the spine, and the middle portion of the padding underneath should rest on the surrounding back muscles. From the side, compare the width of the saddle to your horse's shoulder. Ideally, the saddle should be the same width as his shoulder. Standing by his left shoulder, take your hand and move it in a straight line underneath the saddle. Your hand should easily slide between the horse and the saddle without needing to lift or push it upward. The saddle bars should rest on the sides of the withers and not on the shoulder blades. Attach and adjust the girth or cinch so that two fingers can easily slip between your horse and the front girth. Once the saddle is in place, look down the gullet space toward his tail; you should be able to see right through the space.

Have a helper hold your horse while you mount and position yourself in the saddle. Watch how your horse reacts when you put all of your weight down on the seat. Check your leg position on each side and put your feet into the stirrups. Stand up slightly. As you do, try to insert two fingers between the pommel or gullet and the withers. If you can't do this with ease, the saddle does not fit properly.

If you find a saddle that's got potential and you've cleared it with the tack store, take it for a real test ride. This will give you a good idea how well it performs and feels during a normal ride.

Putting on saddles

The saddle is the first piece of tack to go on your horse. Always be sure to groom your horse prior to putting on a saddle pad. Wipe down the saddle before each use and check to be sure the saddle pad is fairly clean. Your saddle should be set up and ready to be placed on your horse's back. The girths and front cinches should lie over the seat with stirrups run up on the English saddle; on the Western saddle, the tradition is to place the right stirrup around the horn. Remember to tie your horse to a solid object using a quick-release knot. Always begin at your horse's left shoulder.

◆ Place the saddle pad in front of the withers and slide it back with the grain of your horse's hair. Shift the pad so it lies slightly behind the withers and covers the back area. Smooth out the pad.

◆ Hold the saddle with one hand on the pommel or horn and the other hand on the cantle. Lift the saddle up and gently place it on the saddle pad. Do not drop it down or pull it forward.

◆ Grasp the saddle and saddle pad together at the gullet and reposition them. The pair should not be set too far forward on the horse's shoulders. Ideally, you should place it slightly behind the withers.

◆ Once the saddle is in the correct position, move carefully to the other side of your horse and let the girth or front cinch down

Correctly positioned, the English saddle is behind the withers and on the saddle pad.

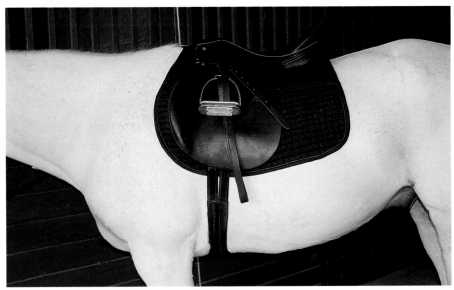

Always perform the two-finger test to make sure the girth is not too loose or too tight. If you can slip two fingers between your horse and the girth with some resistance, the girth is well situated.

slowly from the seat. If using a Western saddle, take the right stirrup off the horn and set it down gently. Move back to the left side of the horse.

◆ Bending down slightly, reach underneath your horse and grab the end of the girth or ask a helper to hand it to you. Never walk under your horse. Set the girth or latigo into the right position down the girth line, about four inches from the elbow. Buckle the girth to the billet straps or cinch up the latigo to secure the saddle in place. Don't make it too tight; check it using the two-finger test. If your horse has a habit of holding his breath when you tighten the cinch or girth (a trick horses learn to avoid tight girths), you'll have to redo it until it fits correctly for your own safety.

Correctly positioning a Western saddle takes practice and good maneuvering skills. This is how it should rest on your horse's back. Take special care when putting the saddle in place and when removing it; do so gently to avoid pinching or bruising your horse's back.

◆ Make sure the girth or latigo is in the right place. If you are planning to put on a breastplate, breastcollar, or martingale, don't tighten them into place yet, just buckle it on a lower billet or cinch strap hole. If putting on a Western saddle, this would be the time to start fitting the flank girth billets in the back.

◆ To remove the saddle, always undo the girth or front cinch first and lay it over the seat. Run the stirrups up or place the right stirrup back over the horn on the Western saddle. Gently lift both the saddle and the saddle pad, moving them back and toward you.

Fitting the bridle and bit

Because the bridle is made up of individual parts you can fit each one to your horse's head and mouth. This versatility guarantees your horse's contentment along with improved rein and hand cues from you. When you put on a new bridle, loosen the straps around it so it can slide on easily. Trying to squeeze your horse's head into the bridle does not benefit you or him. Once you have it on him, begin setting the strap and notches to the desired height and tightness, based on the shape of his head. You shouldn't need to adjust the bridle again unless you are using a different bit or have to refit it after a teeth floating. New leather bridles can be extremely stiff and uncomfortable. Rubbing neat's-foot oil all over them after each wipe down and major cleaning is a great way to soften them.

Putting on the bridle

Have your horse safely tied to a solid object using a quick-release knot. Check his mouth for stray pieces of hay or grass. Put the bridle and reins over your shoulder and approach your horse from his left side. Unbuckle his halter and move it back to his neck. Rebuckle the halter so that it hangs loosely around his neck, still safely tied to a solid object.

Stand at your horse's left shoulder and hold the bridle in your left hand as you place the reins over his head. Allow them to rest on his neck in front of the halter.

Turn your body to face the front of your horse. Place your right hand on the crownband of the bridle while bringing your right arm above his head and between his ears. Press down on the poll to lower your horse's head slightly. Don't lay the crownband or cheekpieces on your horse's face; keep them lifted in a forward position. Move your left hand to hold the bit in front of his mouth.

As you pull the crownband up with your right hand, slip your left

Before putting the bit and bridle on your horse, make sure that you are holding it correctly. Encourage your horse to start lowering his head as soon as your hand is on his poll.

thumb between his lips at the corner of his mouth to aid him in receiving the bit. Pull the bit into his mouth smoothly, making sure he doesn't put his tongue over it.

As the bit sits in your horse's mouth, gently lift the crownband over his ears and manipulate each ear to fit within the space between the crownband and browband.

Loosely buckle the throatlatch to one below the notch that touches your horse's jaw. If he pulls while you're fitting the bridle, it will stay on. Start adjusting the noseband and cheekpieces and check the entire bridle for a comfortable fit (see Fitting the bridle and bit below).

When you're ready to remove the bridle, place the halter and lead rope around your horse's neck and tie him to a solid object using a quick-release knot. First, unbuckle the noseband (if applicable) and then the throatlatch; move the top of the reins forward. Take the reins and the crownband in your right hand and gently pull them together over the ears, slowly lowering the entire bridle down and off his head. Your horse should release the bit as you remove the bridle.

Fitting the bridle and bit

With the bridle on your horse's head, you can align the leather bands in place and check the bit's position in your horse's mouth. Over time, wearing and stretching the leather bridle straps mark the notches you regularly use, making it easier for you to see the correct notch. Have a checklist in your mind as you go through each part of the bridle. Following these steps may help:

◆ Always set the throatlatch at the lowest notch possible. You should be able to fit at least three fingers between it and your horse.

◆ If using an English bridle, position the noseband at the lowest end of the bridge of the nose. Adjust and secure the noseband strap on the cheek side to modify its height; buckle the cavesson noseband at the chin groove. Be sure you can easily slip two fingers between the noseband and your horse.

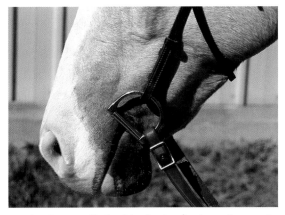

Notice how well the bit sits in the horse's mouth. Only two small creases are visible at the corner, an indication that the bit is at rest within the mouth.

◆ The way the bit sits at the corners of your horse's mouth should allow you to see one or two wrinkles on his lips. The rings of the bit should lie flat and be the only part of the bit visible from the sides. The severity and positioning of the bit can change by altering the height of the cheekpieces. A bit placed too high or low in your horse's mouth can injure his lip and damage his teeth.

Fitting and putting on the blanket

Clipped, shorthaired, and year-round pasture horses must wear some kind of blanket on bitterly cold and snowy days. Because a blanket is usually worn outdoors, it needs to provide a warm, snug fit without interfering with his daily activities. Poorly fitted blankets can cause severe rubbing and lead to hair loss, skin irritations, and infections. An oversized blanket may slip or hang off your horse, endangering him if it gets caught on a fence. It may also cause a severe fall. Take the time to get precise body-length measurements to guarantee a blanket that's comfortable and safe. Although only blankets are mentioned here, sheets can also be fitted and put on using the following instructions:

Measure for body length using a soft measuring tape. The easiest way is to have a helper hold one end of the tape at the center of your horse's chest while you pull the tape in a straight line across one side of your horse to the middle of his tail. This gives you his body length in inches and an exact blanket size. If the body length is an odd number or half size, round it up to the next whole even number.

When you get a new blanket, try it on your horse to make sure it fits and is free of any imperfections. Since most tack stores require that returned purchases be in saleable condition, put a clean, flat bed sheet over your horse before putting on the blanket. The sheet prevents the underside of the blanket from getting dirty and being covered with hair.

Before putting the blanket on your horse's back, fold it in the middle, covering the front half with the back half. The underside of the back half should be facing up because it rests on the front half.

Standing at your horse's left shoulder, gently lay the folded blanket over his withers and move it slightly forward, covering at least two inches of his lower mane. Check that the chest closures are centered in the front.

Extend the back half of the blanket so that it unfolds onto and over your horse's hindquarters.

Once the blanket is flat, walk around your horse to make sure the surcingle and leg straps are down. Straighten out the tail flap.

Fasten the surcingle straps that cross underneath your horse's belly or the girth-surcingle straps that fit around the barrel and fasten them on the horse's left side. Move to the chest closure and fasten the two buckles. If the blanket has leg straps, attach them last.

Once the blanket is on, conduct a thorough inspection, paying special attention to certain areas around the body. At the withers, you

For the best blanket fit, measure your horse using a soft measuring tape, as shown. Start at the middle of his chest and, with a helper, extend the tape along one side of his body to the middle of his tail. The reading in inches will give you the correct blanket size.

should be able to slip a hand between your horse and the blanket. Moving to the shoulder and chest, again, one hand should easily slide between your horse and the blanket. If the blanket has a tail flap, carefully stand on your horse's left side. With your left hand on his stifle, slip your right hand underneath the blanket. With your right hand flat, you should be able to move it around his hind end freely. Also, be sure the blanket or the tail flap isn't so long that it interferes with your horse's ability to raise his tail and defecate. Finally, check the intersecting surcingle straps underneath your horse's belly. Press down lightly on its center with one hand and look at the distance between your hand and the horse. If it looks like more than four inches, you will need to tighten it slightly. A loosely fitted blanket is actually worse than a tight one because of the risk of it falling off or rubbing the skin.

One last blanket test is optional. It requires getting your horse to move around and stretch a little. Have a helper walk your horse for a few minutes and watch to make sure he is walking normally. Stop your horse and look over the blanket; check for any shifting. Put some sweet feed or his favorite treat in a bucket and put it on the ground, inviting your horse to lower his head. Observe whether the blanket rises, pinches, or constricts him around his neck and chest. If possible, gently flex his neck to the sides, looking for any resistance or displacement.

Buying the right tack

Tack stores, mail-order catalogs, online stores, and auctions are excellent outlets for buying new and used tack. Of course, there are advantages and disadvantages to each of these possibilities. Before buying any tack, make a list of what you need and how much you want to spend. Impulse buying is a no-win situation when shopping for tack, and you'll most likely end up buying unnecessary equipment that is way over your budget. Spend some time thinking about the type of riding you're doing or want to do in the future. If you're taking riding lessons, consult your instructor about the kind of tack and equipment you'll need. Ideally, first-time riders should start out using a basic, inexpensive, good-quality tack set and replace it as they advance. Experienced riders need to think more about the long term when deciding on what kind of tack to buy. They may want to consider investing their money in slightly more expensive, top-quality equipment. Once you know what tack you need, review your finances to come up with a realistic and workable budget. With your list and budget in hand, do some comparison shopping.

Tack stores are very hands-on and accommodating to their local horse community. Besides tack, they also sell riding clothes, grooming and healthcare supplies, nutritional supplements, and other horsewear items. Most add a personal touch by taking the time to learn about you, your horse, and your riding interests. Depending on the size of the store, the selection may be limited, but they are usually happy to order items for you directly from the manufacturer. A good number of tack stores sell used tack on consignment and either back their sales up with warranties or have a fair return policy. Buying used tack can be risky if you don't know what you're looking for, but when buying it from a reputable tack store, be assured that the store's owner and staff fully inspected it before they put it on the sales floor. A good rule of thumb is to visit local tack shops first because most of them do what they can to get you what you want at the right price.

The number of people who purchase tack through catalogs has skyrocketed over the past several years. Mail-order companies can offer larger selections at competitive prices because of their relatively lower operating expenses, and they are able to reach horse owners everywhere through their catalogs. Ordering from a catalog by phone, fax, or online can be an easy way to buy most of your tack and supplies. You have a large selection to choose from, often no sales tax, and free shipping specials. When it comes to buying a saddle, many mail-order companies will ship you a loaner saddle for fitting purposes if you give them a credit card deposit. Of course, they have strict return policies for the loaner saddle. Although they'll refund the cost of the saddle, they may not refund the shipping charges. Shipping saddles back and forth can become a very expensive and frustrating ordeal. Check with each mail-order company about its return and refund policies before buying. Their policies may sway your decision on which company you use.

Online stores and auctions are part of the trendy dot.com shopping experience. There are two kinds of online stores: Internet extensions of mail-order companies and independent websites. Independent online tack stores are attractive because they let you select and order from the convenience of your home computer, but as the buyer, you must beware. Although most online tack stores are reputable and stock a significant amount of inventory at excellent prices, you must research the online company fully and find out their return, shipping, and sale policies. Many riders and trainers recommend searching the online tack stores for rare and obscure kinds of tack and equipment.

Online auctions are not as reliable since you're buying from an "invisible" seller, not a legitimate company. You may only have limited recourse if you have a problem. Browsing an online auction is much like shopping at a garage sale. Most of the time the tack is used and sold as-is with no warranties or refunds. Although you may find some inexpensive tack, be careful. It could be severely worn or damaged and not look exactly like the photo. If you shop for your tack online, do it through a reputable store or mail-order company's website. Avoid using the auctions. A better way to buy used tack is through private sales in your local classifieds.

Chapter 7

The Holistic Horse

The earliest form of veterinary medicine was a combination of natural remedies and physiotherapy exercises. As medicine advanced, the holistic approach to curing diseases and injuries faded from the teaching curriculum of most veterinary schools. Younger generations of veterinarians labeled older and unusual practices as "alternative" or "holistic" therapies. This was a deliberate attempt to identify them as optional and nonconventional forms of animal health care, quite apart from establishment veterinary care.

Today, the most commonly practiced equine alternative therapies include acupuncture, chiropractic, massage, hydrotherapy, aromatherapy, flower essences therapy, and herbal supplements. The shared belief behind these therapies is that a horse's emotional and physical state improves through the natural nourishment of his body and mind, not by focusing solely on treating symptoms as modern medicine does. Using a regular regimen of muscle and spinal manipulations, highly fortified diets, relaxation techniques, and methods of enhancing the immune system, holistic therapies embrace the idea that a horse can heal himself and ward off diseases and illnesses. Over the past several years, interest in alternative therapies has markedly increased as horse owners have refused to listen to those dreaded words spoken by many veterinarians, "Not much more we can do." Horse owners often first hear about alternative therapies from fellow owners or barn buddies who have tried a therapy on their own horses. Owners who have seen positive results are usually eager to recommend a specific veterinarian or therapist. Within the equine community, there are two different responses to alternative therapies. One is that of traditional veterinarians and doubtful owners who strongly dispute the effectiveness of alternative therapies, arguing that they thrive on false hopes, double talk, and bias. Another complaint is that they use incomplete studies to cite success. The other view is that of supporters who rebut these claims, emphasizing the proven longevity and popularity of alternative therapies. They ask, if the therapies didn't work, wouldn't the public just stop using them and wouldn't they eventually disappear? Why are they more in demand now than ever before?

Keep in mind that alternative therapies are not miracle cures and that there is no guarantee they will work on your horse. A therapist should never promise an overnight change in your horse. If he or she does, thank them for their time and wave to them as they drive off your property. Alternative therapies reveal their true benefits when sessions are spread over time and provided on a regular basis by an experienced therapist or veterinarian. Even though some traditional and conservative veterinarians attempt to publicly discredit alternative therapies, veterinary associations worldwide have officially recognized acupuncture and chiropractic as credible treatments when performed by board-certified practitioners. As alternative therapies continue to gain respect, many veterinarians are converting their practices into a combination of traditional and alternative medicines to serve a wider range of clients. When considering using any alternative therapy on your horse, read as much as you can about it. Always consult a veterinarian who has a firm understanding of, or experience in, holistic therapies and medications.

Acupuncture

For over four thousand years, the Chinese have used acupuncture to treat and prevent disease and other health conditions in humans and animals. The ancient practice of inserting needles into specific points in the body releases *chi*, or the flow of energy, which improves circulation, stimulates nerve activity, and releases pain-relieving endorphins. In recent years, interest and increased publicity surrounding equine acupuncture has stemmed from the horse racing industry. Horse trainers often were forced to end a horse's racing career due to injuries that didn't respond to typical rehabilitation programs. Word began to spread through the top training barns about injured professional athletes who turned to acupuncture and recovered at faster rates with long-term benefits. Trainers began to ask, If it worked for two-legged athletes, wouldn't it work for four-legged ones?

Many veterinary acupuncturists claim that acupuncture can alleviate pain and pressure, accelerate recuperation from laminitis and tendonitis, effectively clear up aggravating skin conditions, enhance mare and stallion fertility, and even eliminate poor attitude and bad behaviors. Equine acupuncture has been widely praised throughout the sport-horse community for its high success rate in treating the painful

A veterinary acupuncturist inserts special needles into key pressure points on the horse's body to stimulate positive responses and to increase the flow of energy. Credit: Benjamin Espy, DVM © 2003.

and chronic condition of back muscle atrophy due to injuries and to poorly fitting saddles.

The truth is that most horses have a deep fear of needles; their impulse is to run when stuck by one. For everyone's safety, especially the horse, the veterinary acupuncturist might suggest administering a mild sedative before beginning the treatment. Your horse must stand calmly for twenty to thirty minutes while the veterinarian gently inserts sterile needles into the top layer of skin at specific pressure points. Although the needles may cause a slight amount of discomfort initially, the analgesic response kicks in after a few minutes, enabling the horse to relax. The veterinary acupuncturist determines the frequency of acupuncture treatments; the average is one to three treatments per week for about a month. The first signs of improvement usually appear by the third or fourth session. If a positive response continues for a sufficient amount time, the veterinary acupuncturist will begin to lengthen the time between visits. If the condition is a chronic one, he or she may suggest regular appointments two to six times a year. If you are seriously considering using equine acupuncture, consult a certified veterinary acupuncturist or e-mail the American Academy of Veterinary Acupuncture at AAVAOffice@aava.org and visit their website at www.aava.org for a referral.

Chiropractic

A horse depends on his spine for strength and flexibility. If his spinal column is injured or if it is out of alignment, he may experience back pain, lameness, and stiffness. He may also display a poor disposition. An X-ray absolutely confirms the presence of skeletal problems or fractures, but it can't reveal certain musculosketal conditions and injuries that can be just as painful. Chiropractic therapy works by directly manipulating the spinal column into its correct alignment, aiding the transmission of spinal nerve impulses, and relaxing tight connective muscles and ligaments. Veterinarians often use chiropractic in conjunction with acupuncture to loosen and relax the surrounding strained muscles, making it much easier for the veterinary chiropractor to reposition the spine. Make sure the veterinarian doing the adjustment is board certified in equine chiropractic therapy. Be cautious about using human chiropractors who have not been trained or educated in equine musculoskeletal anatomy. An incorrect manipulation could cause severe pain and permanent damage to nerves and tissues.

According to veterinary chiropractors, many common problems respond well to chiropractic therapy. These include gait problems, arthritis, back strain, decreased performance, and traumatic injuries. A

Only a trained veterinarian should perform chiropractic adjustments and manipulations. Distinctive hand techniques and flexion methods are synchronized to realign the horse's spinal column and to release painful tension. Here, Madalyn Ward, DVM of Austin, performs a chiropractic adjustment on the author's horse.

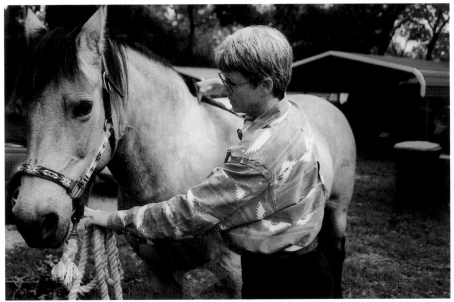

veterinary chiropractor performs a complete evaluation of your horse and carefully reviews your horse's medical history to pinpoint the source of the problem. The number of adjustments depends on various factors, such as your horse's current health, training program, and required performance level. If your horse has an acute back injury or strain due to intense riding or a fall, the veterinarian may first put him on anti-inflammatory medications and stall rest, followed by weekly chiropractic adjustments. Once your horse experiences significant improvements, the veterinarian may reduce the adjustments to every two to three weeks. After a full recovery, you may want to continue monthly chiropractic adjustments as a precaution against injury and relapses and to maintain the strength and suppleness of the spinal region. Most veterinary chiropractors recommend that all active horses have a yearly evaluation and adjustment at least two to three times a year. For chronic conditions, a veterinary chiropractor creates a thorough treatment plan that incorporates chiropractic therapy with complementary therapies, such as acupuncture and massage therapy. To locate a board-certified veterinarian in chiropractic therapy, go to the referral website of the American Veterinary Chiropractic Association at: www.avcadoctors.com

Massage

The ancient Chinese, the Romans, and the Native American Hopis used equine massage therapy in their holistic approach to horsemanship and health care. All massage therapies use specific hands-on techniques to palpate muscles and ligaments. A massage releases spasms, increases circulation, and expels toxins trapped inside muscle tissues. Removing the pain from sore and tense muscles reduces your horse's stress and fear levels, which in turn improves his behavior and learning ability. Most professional trainers agree that a horse that feels great performs better, whether in an arena or on a racetrack. A horse has approximately seven hundred voluntary muscles. This means there are seven hundred possible sore spots, so it's no surprise that a horse's body benefits from regular massage. Underneath the large umbrella of equine massage therapy, there are individual disciplines defined by their distinctive style, procedures, and ideology. Today's most common equine massage techniques include shiatsu, TTouch, sports massage, and Rolfing.

Shiatsu

The Japanese word *shiatsu* means "finger pressure." Shiatsu practitioners believe that the key to good health lies in the balanced energy flow within all living creatures. When anything interferes with that balance, the outcome is a weakened immune system and a higher susceptibility to illnesses. Finger pressures, combined with muscle stretching and limb rotation, return these life-force energies to a healthy and stable equilibrium.

Ttouch

TTouch massage, developed by Linda Tellington-Jones, merges pressure-sensitive touches within a series of fluid circular motions. The massage routine is designed to achieve healing and relaxation, allowing the horse to regain his health, confidence, and self-awareness. TTouch is a vital component of the Tellington-Touch Equine Awareness Method (TTeam) that integrates massage with horse-and-rider collaboration exercises, lessons on balance improvement, and the methodology that allows an owner to communicate on a higher level with his horse.

Sports massage

Sports massage is an intensive deep-muscle workout for the active or athletic horse. It combines finger pressure, hand compressions, and kneading into a pattern of precise arm strokes. Jack Meagher, a sports therapist, developed the original concept and hand technique of massaging racehorses. Over the years, his methods have been modified slightly by equine massage practitioners and schools for use on all types of horses, not just racehorses. The founding principle of the therapy is protecting active horses by maintaining their free motion, thereby preventing deep muscle injuries instead of correcting them.

Rolfing

Dr. Ida Rolf, a biochemist, developed Rolfing, based on fifty years of research. Her teachings stressed the use of articulated patterns of deep massage on connective tissues to return the entire body to a balanced state of improved movement and a complete sense of well-being. Certified Rolfers have highly specialized training in how to use their knuckles and elbows to release strains and tension to achieve what they refer to as "the free flow of movement." Because Rolfing is vigorous and intensive, be patient; your horse may require several sessions to become accustomed to Rolfing and to profit from it.

Selecting a massage therapy

The methods and viewpoints of these massage techniques may be diverse, but their practitioners' commitment is the same: to apply their skills and knowledge to strengthen the horse's body, spirit, and mind. All of them share the notion that a trained hand is the principal tool needed to deliver release and comfort to painfully tight muscles and joints. Educated fingers and palms must apply gentle pressure in a sequence of motions and strokes on the strained muscles of any healthy horse, no matter his age, activity, or breed. More importantly, all the massage techniques are safe. However, they should only be performed according to the individual therapy's criteria for when and when not to massage a horse. The frequency of massages depends on the therapy, and the therapist makes that determination based on several factors, including the primary reason for the massage, a full examination, and any recommendations made by the veterinarian.

Selecting the right kind of massage therapy for your horse is not a simple decision, especially because there are no official regulating or licensing boards that oversee the performance of equine massage therapists. Therefore, you should contact the different equine massage schools and organizations to receive literature and to get referrals for certified therapists in your area. You may also find well-trained and certified practitioners through recommendations from other horse owners at shows and boarding facilities. Always check out a therapist's credentials and education and speak to as many of his or her current clients as possible. The therapist must be properly trained and must possess a comprehensive understanding of equine anatomy, exercise physiology, and the psychology of the horse. All massage therapists must pass a certification test or practical exam through a reputable equine massage program. Again, be wary of human massage therapists who simply wish to break into the equine massage field but lack the necessary experience and education.

The massage therapist should be willing to give you a free consultation, answer all of your questions satisfactorily, and be able to work with the treatment plan designed by a veterinary chiropractor or acupuncturist. If you're still unsure about which type of massage therapy is best for your horse, consult a holistic veterinarian, veterinary chiropractor, or veterinary acupuncturist. To guarantee that your horse is getting the best therapy possible, consider learning how to do equine massage yourself through a certified course or program recommended by a veterinary chiropractor or acupuncturist.

Hydrotherapy

Hydrotherapy, or water therapy, has always been considered the most effective way to alleviate strained muscles and reduce swellings quickly. Veterinarians often prescribe hydrotherapy to control and ease a horse's chronic and acute swellings and strains. They may suggest that you run a hose with cold water up and down the horse's tired, swollen legs or walk him through a deep pond or lake to speed up the healing of lower leg musculoskeletal injuries. The incredible results from these common procedures have inspired many horse trainers to start using special water exercises in their training programs. The natural resistance of water creates a safe and nonrestrictive training environment favorable for strengthening and conditioning muscles and tendons.

Each year the number of equine sporting events and the horses competing in them drastically increases, and so does the rate of injuries and necessary physiotherapy rehabilitations. For a long time, hydrotherapy spas have been extremely helpful in sports-medicine treatments and training programs. Equine researchers in Australia recently determined that hydrotherapy spas accelerated the healing of certain sports-related injuries and significantly shortened the usually drawn-out rest and recovery period required by most veterinarians. The newly designed walk-in equine spa is the next phase in using

Walk-in spas are among the most recent advances in hydrotherapy treatment. Injured horses are able to stand safely inside the spa while cool water streams around their lower legs. Credit: The Centre for Natural Equine Therapy 2003©.

hydrotherapy to treat and prevent severe lower leg injuries. As the horse stands in the spa, cool salt water is agitated around his lower body, reducing painful swelling, increasing oxygen intake, and massaging stiff muscles. Many established equine hospitals and rehabilitation clinics are using hydrotherapy chambers and spas in their postsurgical and physical therapy treatments.

Aromatherapy and flower essences

Deep within the tissues of all plants, there are small sacs filled with volatile substances known as essential oils. These give every plant its distinguishing scent and taste. Known as the "lifeblood" of plants, these therapeutic oils contribute to their ability to ward off disease, absorb water, and reproduce. Essential oils from various forms of plant life, including flowers, berries, grasses, and roots, are extracted through steam distillation. Aromatherapists believe that their therapeutic oil remedies can cure both emotional and physical disorders. Essential oils, blended or in pure form, can be applied topically to infected areas, stirred into feed, massaged into the skin, or inhaled directly. How they are used depends on the type of health problem.

Over the centuries, aromatherapists have recorded the healing properties and medicinal uses of every essential oil. The oils are usually classified by their Latin and common names, major healing activity, and the complaint they treat most often. For instance, tea tree oil, *Melaleuca alternifolia*, is an antifungal and antiseptic agent when used alone or in a remedy formula. It eradicates thrush and ringworm and is an excellent disinfectant for wounds, bites, and burns. True lavender, *Lavandula angustifolia*, is an extremely versatile oil. When inhaled, it can calm horses in stressful situations. It also reduces scarring when applied to a wound topically, and it eases an upset stomach or colic pain when mixed into a tonic.

Aromatherapy remedies are created by blending exact proportions of selected essential oils. Too much or too little of an oil results in an ineffective or harmful elixir. Because these oils are highly potent, you should consult a certified aromatherapist with experience in treating horses before you buy the oils and mix them together haphazardly. Trained aromatherapists can show you exactly how to prepare the oils, teach you how to use them correctly, and help you choose the right oils to improve your horse's health. If hiring an aromatherapist is not in your budget, consider using some of the preblended oils formulated to work on common equine health problems, such as respiratory difficulties, skin conditions, and muscle strains. These ready-to-use oils take the worry out of using essential oils for the first time and are readily available from many horse supply stores, mail-order catalogs, and websites. Be sure to follow the directions exactly as given on the label and packaging. Currently, equine aromatherapy is practiced predominantly in Europe and Australia, but it has gained a strong following in North and South America during the past ten to fifteen years. If you have questions or concerns about aromatherapy for horses, holistic veterinarians are usually familiar with aromatherapy practices and can help you decide if it's right for your horse.

Equine flower essence therapy is based on Dr. Edward Bach's method of utilizing the healing properties of flowers to create an emotional balance within the body. Practitioners of flower essence therapy believe the mind and body are directly connected to one another. When you restore soundness to the mind, the body follows. For example, when a horse experiences fear or anger and acts on it, this negatively affects his immune system and body functions, making him prone to chronic illness and injury. Each of the thirty-eight flowers used in the Bach Flower Essence™ product line, including Cherry Plum, Heather, Holly, and Pine, are harvested from quality-controlled gardens in England. Unlike essential oils, flower essences are almost always produced in liquid form and are less harmful if incorrectly

To treat your horse using aromatherapy, let him inhale the essential oils. Don't insert the bottle in your horse's nostril. Hold it underneath or dab a small amount just below the opening of his nostril.

Flower essences are available in a variety of forms, including topical creams and elixirs. You can find these in dropper or spray bottles to allow for greater versatility in applying them. You can also make a custom spray at home by placing a preblended remedy in a reusable spray bottle.

prepared or used. This means that it is much easier and safer for the typical horse owner to try them. Each flower essence targets distinctive negative behaviors and emotions, so you need to understand which flower essences to combine into a remedy. A remedy blend can contain up to six different flower essences. You use a dropper to administer four drops to the horse's tongue at least four times a day.

For example, if your horse is having spooking problems, acting nervous all the time, and not concentrating during training sessions, you create a remedy of two to four drops of Aspen for the spooking, Impatiens for nervousness, and Chestnut Bud for improving learning abilities mixed with one ounce of purified or distilled water. For the uncooperative horse that refuses to offer his tongue, add a few drops of the remedy or a single-flower essence to his water or feed. Another easy and effective way to administer flower essences is by misting them around your horse using a spray bottle or perfume-diffuser bottle.

In addition to their full line of individual essences, Bach Flower Essence™ produces one premade treatment known as Rescue Remedy®. This unique blend of five flower essences, including Rock Rose and Star of Bethlehem, can calm the fears and nerves of the stressed horse and rider. It is available either as a liquid in a dropper bottle or as a topical cream to be applied on cuts, scrapes, and sores. Many owners include Rescue Remedy® in their first aid kit for minor skin injuries and traumatic situations.

EquiEssences® is another producer of flower essences that specializes in ready-to-use blends for controlling bad behaviors, such as cribbing and aggressiveness, and reinforcing desired behavioral traits, including concentration, compliance, and confidence. If you have questions about how flower essence therapy may affect your horse's health or if you are concerned that it may cause drug interaction problems, speak to a holistic veterinarian, veterinary chiropractor, or veterinary acupuncturist experienced in flower essences therapy.

Herbal supplements

Unlike trees or shrubs that last from year to year, herbs are seed plants whose stems wither each season. For millennia, various cultures have employed herbs as a source of medicine, flavoring, and nutrients. Herbalists believe that ingesting herbs regularly boosts the immune system and empowers the body to heal itself. Because they are herbivores, horses respond positively to herbal supplements and medications. If every horse had access to wild forages and pastures, herbs would become a common ingredient in their grazing diet, delivering healthful benefits on a daily basis. Most herbalists also believe that wild horses keep themselves fit and healthy by seeking out specific herbs in uncultivated fields and forests. Because domesticated horses don't have the luxury of herb-filled pastures, owners can add herbal supplements to their horse's diet.

You can mix selected herbs together into a dry or liquid form and add them to a horse's daily diet to treat specific medical problems, maintain overall health, and improve his emotional well-being. Liquid supplements are much more palatable and quickly absorbed into the horse's digestive system. A horse on liquid supplements usually begins to show improvement within a week. In very rare situations, a horse may dislike the herbal liquid in his feed and refuse to eat it. If this happens after two feedings, you can give the herbal elixir orally, using a plain syringe and releasing the liquid into your horse's throat. This procedure is very similar to giving your horse his wormer paste.

If your horse becomes too stressed from undergoing the syringe method twice a day, consider using dried herbs, which are an excellent alternative. Dry herbs take slightly more time to provide the same results, approximately two to three weeks, because it takes longer to digest them fully, and they are not always completely eaten. Each herb has certain healing characteristics and, when used with complementary herbs, is more powerful and effective than if given separately. For example, Cleavers, *Galium aparine*, is an excellent herbal diuretic principally used for urinary disorders and to stimulate the lymphatic system. Marigold, *Calendula officinalis*, works to relieve digestive problems and ulcers by bringing about stomach muscle contractions and decreasing acidity levels. These two herbs are commonly combined to create an herbal supplement for the maintenance and improvement of the horse's lymphatic system.

Herbalists have spent years researching the capabilities of individual herbs. They know how each herb reacts when used with other herbs, and they have classified each for human, canine, feline, or equine use. You need extensive knowledge and training to diagnose a medical problem and to concoct an herbal medicine to cure it. Although you can buy individual herbs to create personalized blends, the best option for most horse owners is to buy quality supplements that have been strictly formulated for equine diets. Hilton Herbs® is one of the leading manufacturers of equine herbal supplements in the world. They have an extensive selection of liquid and dry herbal blends for various health and emotional concerns. You can purchase their products through mail-order companies or at feed stores that carry organic and natural blends. Discuss using herbal supplements with your veterinarian before buying anything. Although most herbal supplements are a safe and excellent additive to your horse's diet, you should be sure he is not taking medications that could react negatively with any of the herbs. Owners of show and sport horses also need to check with the supplement manufacturer or a veterinarian about the possibility of false positive results on a drug test when using particular herbs.

Understanding alternative therapies and holistic care

The first step in using alternative therapies is to give them a chance to work. If you're skeptical about them, try keeping an open mind to the possible benefits one or all of these therapies could have for your horse. The next step is to learn all you can about the therapy, what it does, how it works, and what the results might be. Do your homework by fully researching the therapies you're interested in before blindly walking into the world of alternative therapies. You can read books dedicated to one type of alternative therapy and learn about its benefits. You can contact each therapy's national association and request all their free informational literature. Most representatives take phone calls and answer your questions right over the phone. The Internet has many sites devoted to equine alternative therapies and therapeutic products. Again, when deciding to use alternative therapies, keep in mind that they are not guaranteed cures. All of them take time to work fully, and the possibility exists that they will have no effect on your horse. Just as in traditional medicine, there are no assurances that these therapies will cure or decrease the severity of your horse's health problems, but they are creditable options worth trying. Because horses are individuals, each responds differently to holistic therapies and medicines and to how long any improvement lasts. Do not make alternative therapies the exclusive source of medical treatments available to your horse. Use them as additional courses of health care, coupled with traditional veterinary medicine. Before starting any alternative therapy, consult your veterinarian or a veterinarian with extensive knowledge in holistic medical care.

Appendix 1: When to Call the Vet

Key: ☠ = Contact veterinarian immediately.

☎ = Contact veterinarian within twelve to twenty-four hours.

Signs or symptoms of illnesses

Bruises ☎ Swelling that doesn't go down after consistent hot and cold treatments may indicate a more severe injury. Anti-inflammatory drugs may be necessary.

Choking ☠ Excessive grunting, heavy salivation, and constant stretching of the neck and head are obvious signs of choking, and horses can't vomit to remove the blockage.

Colic ☠ Symptoms include constant biting at sides, wanting to roll, difficulty defecating or the absence of defecation, and no gut sounds for several hours. Expedient treatment may prevent surgery.

Diarrhea ☠ Blood in the stool or bloody diarrhea may be a sign of a serious condition. Diarrhea or loose manure should be treated within twelve to twenty-four hours.

Eye injuries ☎ Discoloration of the eye and uncontrollable movement of the third eyelid are symptoms of eye problems. Flushed eyes that continue to be irritated or are full of discharge for more than twelve hours may indicate an infection or corneal abrasion.

Fever ☎ Fever over 102 degrees F for twelve hours can indicate an infection.

Fracture ☠ Symptoms include an inability to walk and bone exposure. Many bone fractures require timely surgeries and pain management.

Lameness ☎ Difficulty in walking and placing weight on a leg indicates a problem. Heat from hooves may be the first sign of laminitis.

Off feed ☎ Loss of appetite is not a significant sign unless accompanied by additional symptoms.

Respiratory difficulties ☠ Heaving and noisy breathing can be signs of respiratory distress or disease.

Seizures ☠ Seizures can result from a neurological or metabolic condition and may cause injuries.

Skin infections and disorders ☎ Constant rubbing, biting, and scratching can lead to serious abrasions, bruising, and distress. For proper treatment, the veterinarian must identify the cause of the problem as fungal, yeast, parasitic, or allergen.

Snake bite ☠ Antivenin must be given within a short time or death may occur.

Poisoning ☠ Ingestion of poisonous plants and pesticides and overdoses of medicine must be treated at once or organ failure, systematic paralysis, and death may occur.

Wounds ☠ Wounds that bleed for fifteen minutes or that are obviously more than half an inch deep may require stitches, antibiotics, or surgical procedures for drainage.

Appendix 2: Vaccination and Blood Test Schedule

Infectious diseases and conditions	Prevention plan and vaccinations
Botulism	Optional. Check with your veterinarian if botulism is native to your area. Given once a month for three months. Annual vaccine is required.
Equine distemper (strangles)	Annual intranasal vaccine or series of vaccinations given over a four-week period.
Equine encephalomyelitis	Initial vaccination and then a booster vaccination one month later. Annual vaccine in spring. Vaccine is combined with tetanus vaccine.
Equine infectious anemia (EIA)	Annual Coggins blood test required. Infected horses must be quarantined.
Equine influenza	Initial vaccination and then a booster vaccination one month later. Booster vaccinations must be given every six months.
Potomac horse fever (PHF)	Initial vaccination, preferably before the summer, and then a booster vaccination one month later. Horses in endemic areas should receive a booster vaccine every six months. All other horses should receive an annual vaccine.
Rabies	Initial vaccination and then a booster vaccination one month later. Annual vaccine is required.
Rhinopneumonitis (Herpes viruses)	Annual vaccine for all horses. Pregnant mares must receive additional boosters in the fifth, seventh, and ninth month of gestation in addition to their yearly booster.

Tetanus	Initial vaccination in stages: two to three doses over an eight-week period. Annual vaccine is required.
West Nile virus (WNV)	Given in two doses within a four-to eight-week period and repeated yearly. Vaccinations must be completed at least one month prior to mosquito season.

(Note: This is only a suggested vaccination and blood test schedule. Always consult a veterinarian for the best course of treatment and prevention for your horse.)

Appendix 3: The Body Condition Score System[1]

Score	Description
1	**Poor.** The horse is emaciated. The spinous processes (backbone), ribs, tailhead, hooks and pins all project prominently. The bone structures of the withers, shoulders, and neck are easily noticeable, and no fat can be felt anywhere.
2	**Very Thin.** The spinous processes are prominent. The ribs, tailhead, and pelvic bones stand out, and bone structures of the withers, neck, and shoulder are faintly discernable.
3	**Thin.** The spinous processes stand out, but fat covers them to midpoint. Very slight fat cover can be felt over the ribs, but the spinous processes and ribs are easily discernable. The tailhead is prominent, but individual vertebrae cannot be seen. Hook bones are visible but appear rounded. Pin bones cannot be seen. The withers, shoulders, and neck are accentuated.
4	**Moderately Thin.** The horse has a negative crease along its back, and the outline of the ribs can just be seen. Fat can be felt around the tailhead. The hook bones cannot be seen, and the withers, neck, and shoulders do not look obviously thin.
5*	**Moderate.** The back is level. Ribs cannot be seen but are easily felt. Fat around the tailhead feels slightly spongy. The withers look rounded, and the shoulder and neck blend smoothly into the body.
6*	**Moderate to Fleshy.** There may be a slight crease down the back. Fat around the tailhead feels soft, and the fat over the ribs feels spongy. There are small deposits along the sides of the withers, behind the shoulders, and along the sides of the neck.

7   **Fleshy.** There may be a crease down the back. Individual ribs can be felt, but there is noticeable fat between the ribs. Fat around the tailhead is soft. Fat is noticeable in the withers, the neck, and behind the shoulders.

8   **Fat.** The horse has a crease down the back. Spaces between the ribs are so filled with fat that the ribs are difficult to feel. The area along the withers is filled with fat, and fat around the tailhead feels very soft. The space behind the shoulders is filled in flush, and some fat is deposited along the inner buttocks.

Score   Description
9   **Extremely Fat.** The crease down the back is very obvious. Fat appears in patches over the ribs, and there is bulging fat around the tailhead, withers, shoulders, and neck. Fat along the inner buttocks may cause buttocks to rub together, and the flank is filled in flush.

* = The ideal body condition score for broodmares is between 5 and 6.

[1] The condition scoring system described herein was developed by D.R. Henneke and co-workers in the Equine Science section, Department of Animal Science, Texas A&M University, in 1981.

Appendix 4: Forms for Keeping Records

Information Sheet

Horse's name _____

Breed _____

Registration number _____

Date of birth _____

Sex (circle one):   Mare   Stallion   Gelding

Height _____

Weight _____

Color _____

Special markings _____

Tatoos or brands _____

In Case of Emergency

Primary contact _____

Telephone numbers _____

Cell phone numbers _____

Secondary contact _____

Telephone numbers _____

Cell phone numbers _____

Veterinarian _____

Telephone numbers_____

Cell and pager numbers _____

Allergies and medical conditions _____

_____

General Health and Worming Record

Horse's name _____

Date of birth _____

Veterinarian's name _____

Veterinarian's telephone and pager numbers _____

_____

Vaccination	Date	Wormer used	Date	Misc. vet visit	Date
_____	____	_____	____	_____	____
_____	____	_____	____	_____	____
_____	____	_____	____	_____	____
_____	____	_____	____	_____	____
_____	____	_____	____	_____	____
_____	____	_____	____	_____	____
_____	____	_____	____	_____	____
_____	____	_____	____	_____	____
_____	____	_____	____	_____	____
_____	____	_____	____	_____	____
_____	____	_____	____	_____	____
_____	____	_____	____	_____	____
_____	____	_____	____	_____	____
_____	____	_____	____	_____	____
_____	____	_____	____	_____	____

Shoeing Record

Horse's name_____

Date and year _____

Farrier's name	Service	Amount paid	Date
_____	_____	_____	_____
_____	_____	_____	_____
_____	_____	_____	_____
_____	_____	_____	_____
_____	_____	_____	_____
_____	_____	_____	_____
_____	_____	_____	_____
_____	_____	_____	_____
_____	_____	_____	_____
_____	_____	_____	_____
_____	_____	_____	_____
_____	_____	_____	_____
_____	_____	_____	_____
_____	_____	_____	_____
_____	_____	_____	_____
_____	_____	_____	_____
_____	_____	_____	_____
_____	_____	_____	_____
_____	_____	_____	_____
_____	_____	_____	_____

Boarding Services Record

Horse's name _____

Stable manager's name _____

Telephone number _____

Monthly payment due date _____

Boarding services	Billing date(s)	Charges/Fees	Date paid/Check #
_____	_____	_____	_____
_____	_____	_____	_____
_____	_____	_____	_____
_____	_____	_____	_____
_____	_____	_____	_____
_____	_____	_____	_____
_____	_____	_____	_____
_____	_____	_____	_____
_____	_____	_____	_____
_____	_____	_____	_____
_____	_____	_____	_____
_____	_____	_____	_____
_____	_____	_____	_____
_____	_____	_____	_____
_____	_____	_____	_____
_____	_____	_____	_____
_____	_____	_____	_____
_____	_____	_____	_____
_____	_____	_____	_____

Monthly Expense Record

Horse's name _____

Month and year _____

Owner's name _____

Date	Payee's name	Item/Services rendered	Amount
_____	_____	_____	_____
_____	_____	_____	_____
_____	_____	_____	_____
_____	_____	_____	_____
_____	_____	_____	_____
_____	_____	_____	_____
_____	_____	_____	_____
_____	_____	_____	_____
_____	_____	_____	_____
_____	_____	_____	_____
_____	_____	_____	_____
_____	_____	_____	_____
_____	_____	_____	_____
_____	_____	_____	_____
_____	_____	_____	_____
_____	_____	_____	_____
_____	_____	_____	_____
_____	_____	_____	_____

TOTAL:

Index